# MURRAY WALKER'S

## FORMULA ONE HEROES

Dear Reader,

As this updated edition of my book is published in October 2001, I will – with deep regret – just have done my last Formula One television commentary. Fifty-three years – for that is what it has been – is a long time for anything, but for commentating on one sport it is a very long time!

When I reported to my BBC Radio producer for the British Grand Prix at Silverstone in 1949 (no TV coverage in those days), Stirling Moss was a boy and the cars I was going to be talking about had their engines at the front. The drivers wore short-sleeved T-shirts, linen trousers and fabric skull-caps. They had no safety belts, the cars were mobile death traps that were – in effect – high-powered petrol tanks with absolutely no crash protection, and the massive crowd was separated from the projectiles on the track by a piece of rope. There were no barriers, no gravel traps and the medical facilities were minimal.

Things are very different now, with safety improved beyond recognition, all the slick sophistication of pit-stops, digital timing, luxurious motor homes, fast-moving and high-stepping promotion, electronics everywhere, superb presentation and, thanks to the miracle of television, the ability to watch the racing, live and in real time, from anywhere in the world. It has been my enormous privilege to see it all happen, to work with some wonderful people, watch and talk about motor racing's greats and marvel at their cars. I am going to miss it more than I can say.

But time waits for no man, and it certainly isn't going to wait for me. We all deteriorate and I am no exception, which is why I have always been determined to stop while I am still ahead with the viewers, rather than hang on until they think I'm past it. I just have a gut feeling that now is the time to wind down. So farewell but not goodbye and, from the bottom of my heart, my thanks and gratitude to all the wonderful people in motor sport who have made my life such a joy, particularly the fans on the other side of the track whose enthusiasm and friendship have supported me over the years.

Read on and you'll see who my Heroes have been, but the beauty of this truly great sport is that, as it develops, there will be plenty more to come!

This edition published in 2001 by
Virgin Books Ltd
Thames Wharf Studios
Rainville Road
London W6 9HA

Reprinted, 2001 (3 times)

First published in 2000 by Virgin Publishing

A catalogue record for the book is available from
the British Library.

ISBN 1 85227 918 4

Art direction and design by Derek Slatter and
Katherine Spokes at Slatter-Anderson.

Printed and bound by The Bath Press, Bath

# MURRAY WALKER'S
## FORMULA ONE HEROES

### MURRAY WALKER
### & SIMON TAYLOR

# CONTENTS

# *Introduction*

I guess it is true to say that my addiction to motor sport is an inherited genes thing. For would I have had this passion if I'd been the son of a plumber? Who knows, but I doubt it.

My beloved father, Graham Walker, was a kind, generous, cheerful and friendly man with a wonderful way with words and a personality the size of a house. In World War One he was a despatch rider. Thereafter he made a very healthy living racing motorcycles for some 15 years, and was a truly great competitor. Riding for Norton, Sunbeam and Rudge-Whitworth - all now sadly just memories from Britain's great two-wheeled racing past - he won the Isle of Man TT when it mattered more than all the other top races put together. He was the first home in many international Grands Prix, captained the winning British team in the prestigious International Six Days Trial (in which I was, much later, proudly to win a Gold Medal myself), and was one of the greatest motorcycling all-rounders the world has ever seen.

All this was happening from the time I was born in 1923 until only a few years before I left school. So, growing up in my famous father's shadow, I was likely either to love or to loathe motor sport. Actually, I was fairly unaffected by my unusual childhood because his dramatic occupation didn't strike me as being anything out of the ordinary. It was just what he did.

But the bug had bitten. All those idyllic holidays in the Isle of Man, Ulster, Holland, Belgium, Austria, Germany, Spain and France

**Above:** Nine-year-old Murray Walker stands proudly beside his father Graham, who has just finished second in the 1932 Isle of Man Lightweight TT on his 250cc Rudge-Whitworth.

**Far right:** Before my last British Grand Prix commentary for BBC TV in 1996, Bernie Ecclestone invited me to join Williams team-mates Jacques Villeneuve and Damon Hill in the drivers' pre-race parade in a Rolls-Royce Silver Ghost. Jacques won the race, but I already had the flowers!

watching my Dad winning races and being the hero of the crowds had their effect. When World War Two ended I left the army and took up motorcycle racing myself, in the fond belief that I'd show the Old Man how it should really be done.

Wrong! I wasn't nearly good enough, and anyway I was preoccupied with trying to build a successful career in the advertising business. So, after winning a heat at Brands Hatch (then an anti-clockwise *grass* track) on a 250cc AJS, I gracefully retired at the top of my inadequate form to comply with the old adage, "Those that can, do. Those that can't, talk about it!"

Again I was following in my father's footsteps, for when he left the saddle he became a great broadcaster whose radio commentaries from the TT course that he knew so well were the stuff of legend. For the 14 years until his death in 1962 we were the BBC's motorcycle commentary team and, in time, that led to my becoming its Formula One man.

But not for quite a while. Until 1978 I was primarily a bike chap who was also a gigantic car racing enthusiast. Motorcycle road races, trials and scrambles, I did them all, on radio and TV for the BBC, and on TV for ITV. Gradually I got into the car scene as well by way of rallycross, Formula Ford, Formula 3 and Touring Cars, with the occasional Formula One event to whet my appetite: like the 1969 German Grand Prix at the stunning original Nürburgring, when Jacky Ickx took his Brabham to victory, and the Ring again in 1974 for Clay Regazzoni's memorable Ferrari win.

And then in 1978 Jonathan Martin, BBC TV's Head of Sport, sent for me and said: "Murray, we're now going to do all the Formula One rounds, and I want you to handle the

**Above:** The start of my first-ever commentary for BBC Radio, the 1949 British Grand Prix at Silverstone. On the five-car front row are, from left, Villoresi and Bira (Maseratis), Walker (ERA), winner de Graffenried (Maserati) and Gerard (ERA).

commentary." Yes sir! Yes indeed!

Fifty-two years have now passed since my first-ever BBC commentary on the 1949 British Grand Prix at Silverstone, and 23 years since I was lucky enough to become TV's Formula One commentator. I can look back on a wonderfully happy life which has taken me round the world umpteen times as an enthusiastic and excited observer of the sport I love so much.

Motorcycles? Those immortals Jimmy Guthrie, Tim Hunt, Stanley Woods, Jimmy Simpson and Wal Handley were family friends, and my childhood "uncles" when we all stayed at the Castle Mona Hotel in Douglas for the Isle of Man TT races which, for me, still have a magic beyond words. Geoff Duke, Mike Hailwood, Phil Read, Giacomo Agostini, Jim Redman, John Surtees, Barry Sheene, Wayne Gardner and the other later greats were a lot more to me than just the people I revered and respected as some of the

greatest of all time. They were my friends.

Luck plays a major part in everybody's life, and I was privileged to be associated in a small way with Germany's world-beating Mercedes-Benz and Auto-Union teams when they came to England in 1937 and 1938 for the Donington Grands Prix. So I can put my hand on my heart and say, with truth, that I've stood beside Tazio Nuvolari, Bernd Rosemeyer, Rudolf Caracciola, Hermann Lang and the autocratic Manfred von Brauchitsch, and marvelled at their spectacular driving of the dominant, brutal silver-coloured high-tech monsters.

And since 1949, by virtue of my broadcasting life, I've been fortunate enough to have been where it's at as worldwide motor sport developed from its modest post-war beginnings to its current worldwide eminence. Do I appreciate my luck? I most certainly do, and I never cease to marvel at it. I've been massively privileged to meet and know so many great people, not just the drivers and riders but the officials, industry leaders and workers, the engineers, mechanics, sponsors, media people, enthusiasts and countless others who make motor sport so exciting and absorbing.

Time, then, to share my thoughts. Who were my true heroes? The drivers, the personalities and the folk behind the scenes: who were the people who have made the sport what it is? All will be revealed, but I must emphasise that they are *my* heroes, and also that I have not attempted to rank them in any order of absolute merit. That would have to be a very subjective affair when you're covering a period of over half a century.

Your own personal "Greats" may well be very different to mine. Was Fangio "greater" than Senna? Clark "greater" than Schumacher? Ascari "greater" than Prost? Each raced at different times to very different regulations, in very different cars, in very different circumstances and on very different circuits.

So I've chickened out. I have my views, of course. For me the fire, the style, the charisma, the all-round brilliance and the sheer ability to win races against overwhelming odds puts Tazio Nuvolari above all others, in the same way and for the same reasons that my friend the late Mike Hailwood is my all-time Number One motorcycle hero. But I can't prove it. It's not a mathematical or logical thing. It's a gut feeling based on my personal preferences and bias. I've simply

wandered down memory lane decade by decade, recalling the men and their feats who have meant the most to me. And I've slipped in a trio of circuits where my commentating adrenaline has flowed most freely. Not that it takes much to get it going anywhere!

I've cheated a bit, too. I've called this book *Murray Walker's Formula One Heroes*, so I'd better come clean about the fact that three of my heroes - Nuvolari, Caracciola and Rosemeyer - were pre-war aces and therefore never raced in the Formula

One World Championship. They're in simply because, Formula One or not, they're my heroes, and I couldn't bear to leave them out. So should I have included the great Christian Lautenschlager, who brilliantly won both the 1914 and 1918 French Grands Prix for Mercedes-Benz, and who was just as much a top man of his era as my heroes were of theirs? Maybe: but that would, I think, be going a step too far!

So read on and, agree or not, I hope you enjoy what's turned me on for all these years, and will continue to do so until I clamber into that great commentary box in the sky.

**Above:** Caracciola at speed in the 1938 Grand Prix Mercedes-Benz, the four-cam V12 W154, built to the new 3-litre formula. With this car he won the Swiss Grand Prix and the Coppa Acerbo at Pescara.

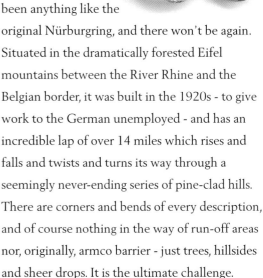

Right: The inscription inside the left-hand ring reads: *Sieger im Grohsen Preis von Europa 1927* (Winner of the 1927 European Grand Prix), the first major motor-cycle race to be held on the fabled Nürburgring in Germany's Eifel mountains. To win it on his 500cc Sunbeam my father took over five and a half hours to cover 18 laps of the demanding 17.6-mile circuit. His ride to victory on his 500cc Rudge-Whitworth in the 15-lap 1930 German GP took him four hours. And he still looked fresh and cheerful!

The concept of a worldwide international top class of racing - Formula One - was only dreamed up by the FIA in 1947, and until 1950 there was no World Championship. But there had been great motor sport for more than half a century before that. The first major races around the turn of the century were incredible city-to-city affairs across Europe, danger-laden battles through the dust in immense, crude Edwardian racers. The French ran the first Grand Prix in 1906, and the 1914 French GP, with its titanic struggle between Georges Boillot's Peugeot and Christian Lautenschlager's Mercedes, was one of the greatest races of all time.

But for the young and impressionable Murray Walker, the 1930s was a decade of unparalleled glamour and motor racing magic. For they were the legendary times of Tazio Nuvolari, Rudolf Caracciola and Bernd Rosemeyer, and of

the Ring at its best.

There's never been anything like the original Nürburgring, and there won't be again. Situated in the dramatically forested Eifel mountains between the River Rhine and the Belgian border, it was built in the 1920s - to give work to the German unemployed - and has an incredible lap of over 14 miles which rises and falls and twists and turns its way through a seemingly never-ending series of pine-clad hills. There are corners and bends of every description, and of course nothing in the way of run-off areas nor, originally, armco barrier - just trees, hillsides and sheer drops. It is the ultimate challenge.

And here I have to declare a special interest, for my father Graham Walker won the first-ever motorcycle Grand Prix at the Nürburgring in 1927 - it lasted for over five and a half hours! - and then won it again in 1930. I still have the two magnificent gold rings that were part of his prize. Sadly, use of the full circuit was discontinued for Grands Prix for safety reasons after Niki Lauda was nearly killed there in 1976, but lesser events are still held on the old Ring, and for a small fee you can drive round in your road car.

To win at the Ring you

the fabled circuit where they had some of their finest victories: the Nürburgring. It was a long time before Formula One, but it was a halcyon period, and I feel privileged to have seen these historic superstars at work, and to have known

had to be special, and it's no coincidence that my three pre-war heroes all turned in towering drives around that daunting and unfriendly track. None more so than the man I've already named my all-time racing hero, Tazio Nuvolari.

**Above**: The all-conquering 1932 Alfa Romeo team was run under the banner of Scuderia Ferrari. Drivers Baconin Borzacchini and Tazio Nuvolari flank a rarely smiling Enzo Ferrari.

He was born in 1892 in a village not far from the northern Italian town of Mantua, and throughout his career he was known as *Il Mantovano Volante* - the Flying Mantuan. "Charisma" is a pretty hackneyed word these days, but no-one has ever had more than the fiery Nuvolari. Short, dark and wiry, he had a unique driving style, all energy, aggression and determined forcefulness, flinging his car into lurid four-wheel drifts, making non-stop steering corrections and literally willing it on to victory - even to the extent of beating his fist on the side of the cockpit to urge it on. In a red leather skull cap, blue cotton trousers and his traditional yellow pullover with a leather waistcoat on top, he was as colourful as his driving style, and one of the most versatile and successful drivers of all time.

Tazio was small and fearless, and the first of a lifetime of broken bones came from falling off a horse as a small boy. World War One delayed his start in motor sport, and he was in his late twenties when he began racing motorcycles. His

first recorded success in a car was fourth at Lake Garda in 1921 in an Ansaldo, but he continued to split his energies between two and four wheels. Soon he was one of Europe's top riders, becoming 500cc champion of Italy in 1924. In 1925 he was given a trial in a P2 Alfa Romeo at Monza but crashed when the gearbox seized - and a week later, heavily bandaged, he was lifted on to his Bianchi motorcycle to won the Grand Prix des Nations in pouring rain. After five wins in a self-financed Bugatti, he switched to Alfa Romeo and was second to Varzi at Leghorn in 1929 - this time driving with his ribs in plaster because he'd crashed his Bianchi motorbike on the same circuit the previous week! This theme of almost

in sports cars, winning the legendary Mille Miglia and Targa Florio road races, the Le Mans 24 Hours and, in appalling conditions, the Tourist Trophy, in an MG Magnette.

But his finest hour was at the Nürburgring, in the 1935 German Grand Prix. Aged 43, and in an outdated Scuderia Ferrari 3.8-litre P3 Alfa, he defeated the combined might of the magnificent Mercedes-Benz and Auto-Union teams with sheer skill and bravura, to the dismay of the 400,000 Germans who had come to see their cars dominate! Delayed by a long stop when his refuelling rig broke, he nevertheless stormed back up the field to score an unforgettable victory. In 1936 he beat the silver cars three more times, in

**Far left**: Bernd Rosemeyer came from motorcycle racing straight to a brilliant career at Auto Union, and the rear-engined monsters were the only cars he ever raced up to his tragically premature death aged 28.

**Left**: In a race of unrivalled drama my all-time hero Tazio Nuvolari defeated the combined might of the Mercedes-Benz and Auto-Union teams, including Rudolf Caracciola and Bernd Rosemeyer, to win the 22-lap, 312-mile German GP at the fabled Nürburgring in his outdated Alfa-Romeo P3. A truly heroic achievement.

simultaneous heroism on two wheels and four is echoed later by two more of my heroes, John Surtees and Mike Hailwood.

By the end of 1930 Nuvolari had forsaken motorcycles to concentrate fully on racing cars. He drove Scuderia Ferrari's Alfa Romeos to a string of victories, and also drove for the Maserati and Bugatti works teams. Not only a mighty force in Grand Prix racing, he was even more successful

Hungary, Spain and Milan, and not surprisingly Auto Union came after him in mid-1937 to join their mighty team.

Which is how I came to see, on a memorable day in late October 1938, one of motor-racing's legends at his brilliant best. The Donington Grand Prix twice attracted the all-conquering Auto Union and Mercedes-Benz teams, and the second of those occasions gave me the indelible memory

**Above:** Rudi Caracciola led the Mercedes-Benz team throughout their six mighty seasons before World War Two, and a string of victories made him Champion of Europe in 1935, 1937 and 1938.

of the Flying Mantuan, a tiny yellow-jerseyed figure bouncing up and down in the cockpit of his huge Auto Union, scoring a great victory ahead of the Mercedes of Hermann Lang and Dick Seaman.

After the war Nuvolari raced on, winning the Albi GP for Maserati aged 54, and leading the Mille Miglia before a misfire dropped him to second. The courage and fire were undimmed, but he was now a sick man, driving in the Milan GP one-handed holding a blood-soaked handkerchief over his mouth. He died in Mantua in 1953, just after his 61st birthday.

That day at Donington in 1938 I also watched Rudolf Caracciola race, and his autograph is one of my treasured possessions. Caracciola was to the 1930s, when the Mercedes-Benz Silver Arrows ruled the roost, what Senna, Prost and Schumacher were to their eras. Nuvolari won the German Grand Prix once, but Caracciola won it five times. He was also a multiple hillclimb champion - at a time when this was a very prestigious part of the sport - and a prolific record-breaker. When the track was wet he was well-nigh unbeatable: he was the acknowledged Rainmaster of his day.

Good-looking, masterful, cheerful but

modest, Caracciola was Germany's idol, and although he raced other makes of car - notably Alfa Romeo - he *was* Mercedes-Benz. He was Stuttgart's Number One from their dramatic return to Grand Prix racing in 1934 until World War Two stopped the sport for a far bigger contest of the nations. Lang, Seaman, von Brauchitsch, Nuvolari, Varzi and Rosemeyer: Rudolf Caracciola beat them all. After the war he made a couple of attempts to return to racing, but each time massive accidents ended his efforts. He died in 1959 at the early age of 58, and remains one of the very greatest of all time. And very much one of my personal heroes.

Where Caracciola's career was long and distinguished, that of Bernd Rosemeyer burned with brilliant intensity for a tragically short time. A handsome, happy-go-lucky, fair-haired German, he came from Lingen, near the Dutch border, and like Nuvolari (and later Ascari, Surtees, Hailwood and Damon Hill), he started his motor sport career as a very successful motorcycle racer, riding for the all-conquering DKW two-stroke team. But in 1935 he switched to four wheels, to become a junior member of the new Auto Union organisation.

As someone who had never driven a front-engined racing car, Rosemeyer possessed a unique attribute. He simply didn't realise how tremendously difficult the powerful and immensely tail-happy 16-cylinder Auto Union was to drive! With incredible reflexes and a massive will to win, he mastered the car in a way that no-one else, even Nuvolari, ever managed to do.

His second race with this treacherous car was the Eifelrennen at the equally treacherous Nürburgring, and he disputed the lead with Caracciola in a great battle before taking victory.

He was only to live for two more seasons, but he made them unforgettable, with demonstrations of unique driving brilliance and a string of magnificent victories. He won the Eifelrennen in 1936, in thick mist which seemed not to slow him one iota, and to underline his special skill at the Nürburgring he took the German Grand Prix that year also, and the Eifelrennen again in 1937. He never raced any other car except the Auto Union, but in three short seasons he became their greatest pilot.

As a 14-year-old schoolboy I was able to accompany the Mercedes-Benz and Auto-Union entourage to Donington, because a family friend was their English interpreter. I watched spellbound as Rosemeyer won that 1937 Donington Grand Prix, which had such a massive impact on Grand Prix-starved Britain. If I'd have known that, three months later, he was to die during a record attempt when his Auto Union streamliner was blown off the Frankfurt-Darmstadt autobahn at 270 mph by a gust of wind, I'd have been distraught. Rosemeyer was just 28. How does the saying go? Those they love the gods take early. They certainly did with Bernd Rosemeyer.

**Below:** The V16, six-litre Auto Union was a real handful around the narrow, twisty lanes of Donington Park, but Rosemeyer averaged over 82 mph for more than three hours to win the 1937 race, ahead of Mercedes-Benz drivers von Brauchitsch and Caracciola.

21

# *Juan Manuel* FANGIO

- *The only man to win five World titles, despite being nearly 38 when he first came to Europe to race against international opposition*

- *Total superiority over his generation of drivers - in sheer driving ability, and in strategic thinking. Held in great respect by those he raced against*

- *Courteous and gentlemanly manner hiding a steely determination and extraordinary stamina, honed by early drives in South American long-distance races*

## FACTS

**Born**: Balcarce, Argentina, 24 June 1911
**Died**: Balcarce, Argentina, 17 July 1995
**Grands Prix**: 51
**First Grand Prix**: Silverstone 1950, Alfa Romeo
**Last Grand Prix**: Reims 1958, Maserati
**Wins**: 24
**Pole positions**: 29
**Points**: 277.14
**Points per start**: 5.43
**Percentage wins**: 47%
**World Champion**: 1951, Alfa; 1954, Maserati/Mercedes; 1955, Mercedes; 1956, Ferrari; 1957, Maserati

I've already said I'm not keen on putting my Formula One heroes into any absolute order of merit. Cars, rules, technology and the sport as a whole have changed out of all recognition over the past half-century, and so has the job of a racing driver. It hasn't necessarily got easier or more difficult: it's just different. That's why you can't say whether Moss was better than Prost, or Senna better than Clark.

Mind you, that doesn't stop people constantly asking me to do exactly that. And, when I presented a TV programme a few years ago which required me to nominate my all-time Top Ten, the man whom I unhesitatingly put at the top of the list was a quiet Argentinian with cool, piercing eyes called Juan Manuel Fangio.

The statistics don't tell half the story, but even on their own they're devastating. In seven full seasons of Formula One, Fangio was World Champion five times, and runner-up twice. No-one, before or since, has demonstrated that kind of superiority over that length of time in Formula One, and I don't believe anyone ever will.

While there were other non-championship F1 races on the calendar in those days, when the World Championship started there were barely half a dozen rounds a season, which is why in his whole career Fangio only contested just 51 points-scoring Grands Prix. He qualified on the front row for 48 of them, and 29 times he took pole position. His tally reads 24 wins, 10 seconds, a third, five fourths and 11 retirements: incredibly, he never finished lower than fourth. He won 47.6 per cent of his races, a record that will surely never be beaten. Compare it with Jackie Stewart

on 27 per cent, or Alain Prost and Ayrton Senna on 25 per cent, and you realise that this man *never* had a bad day.

Fangio was already nearly 39 years old when I watched him take part in the first-ever World Championship round at Silverstone in May 1950, driving for the works Alfa Romeo team. I remember feeling overwhelmed by the superiority and professionalism of the whole team, with their thunderous straight-eight supercharged 158s, and seeing this calm, stocky, balding man in the middle of it all, with his slightly bandy legs and the penetrating glance of his pale blue eyes. Later I watched him race at Silverstone and Aintree in Maserati 250F, Mercedes-Benz W196 and Ferrari cars, and he was always the class of the field. Formula One wasn't on TV in those days, so as an enthusiast rather than a broadcaster I worshipped him from afar (although it was easy for enthusiasts to get into the paddock in those days!). He retired in 1957, aged 46, and lived on into his eighties, a revered figure.

*Right*: Throughout his F1 career, Fangio's domination of Grand Prix racing earned him the unquestioning respect of his fellow drivers.

During his retirement I met him several times, and discovered for myself that he was indeed the true gentleman that legend had led me to expect. In 1987 I filmed a long interview with him. He only spoke Italian and his native Spanish, so we were talking through an interpreter, but I was astounded by his total recall and also, I have to say, somewhat overawed in the presence of so charismatic a hero. To hear in his own voice the stories of those great drives that were the stuff of legend was an extraordinary experience. Even in old age the light in those eyes hadn't dimmed, and you realised that, gentleman he may have been, but he'd trodden a hard and determined road to become the best in the world.

When he was born, of humble parents in the small Argentinian town of Balcarce, there was no silver spoon in his mouth. A self-taught mechanic, he found fame in his homeland driving ancient self-prepared American sedans in those amazing South American road races that traversed the continent and lasted for days at a time. It was

After he won the biggest of all the cross-country races, the 6000-mile Gran Premio del Norte from Argentina through Bolivia to Peru and back, the Peron government saw in him a potential national hero who could fly the Argentinian flag around the world. So they advanced the necessary finances for the Argentinian Automobile Club to buy a Maserati for him, and send him to Europe for the 1949 season. At first the racing establishment looked upon this South American interloper, this self-taught mechanic, with disdain and some resentment, but that didn't shake Fangio's courteous calm. He let the results do the talking. On that first visit to Europe he won his first four races on the trot, and then two more, and before long his tremendous speed and style had earned him a seat with the best Grand Prix team of the day, Alfa Romeo.

Fangio did two years for Alfa, earning his first World Championship title in 1951. But then he missed virtually the whole 1952 season because of the only bad accident he had in all his career. Typically, the accident happened because of his overwhelming determination to race. In those days F1 drivers didn't just compete in F1: they raced sports cars, *formule libre*, touring cars, and anything else that took their fancy. So, hard though it seems to comprehend today, Fangio was entered to drive the V16 BRM in a race in Dundrod, Ireland, on the Saturday, and a Maserati in a minor race at Monza on the Sunday.

Air travel was more of an undertaking half a century ago. On the Saturday evening Fangio flew

**Above:** Fangio hustles the Alfa Romeo 158 around Silverstone in the first round of the first season of the World Championship, the 1950 British Grand Prix. It was a rare fruitless day: a broken oil line led to engine failure.

in those gruelling events that he developed the extraordinary stamina and depths of resourcefulness that were to stand him in good stead throughout his international career.

from Belfast to Paris, but fog prevented him making the onward connection to Rome. No motorways then, either, but he borrowed a car and drove through the night, south to Italy. He drove into the Monza paddock an hour before the race began, and started from the back of the grid. Exhausted, he made a rare misjudgement at Lesmo Corner on lap 2 and his car cartwheeled off the track, leaving him with a broken neck and severe head injuries. He was out of racing for the rest of the year, and blamed himself for the accident. Never again would he attempt two races in two different countries in two days.

Returning from his injuries at the start of 1953, he found Ascari sweeping all before him in the strong, reliable Ferrari 500. But, in the more fragile Maserati, he out-qualified Ascari to take pole at those two dauntingly fast road circuits, Spa and Berne, and won the last race of the year at Monza to finish runner-up in the Championship.

From then on he was to reign as uninterrupted Champion for four years. By the end of 1952 it was an open secret that Mercedes-Benz were planning a return to Grand Prix racing. Their legendary team manager Alfred Neubauer wanted the best of everything, so naturally he approached Fangio. But the German cars weren't ready until Round 3 of 1954, so Fangio did the first two rounds that year in a Maserati, and won both of them. Then, for the French Grand Prix at Reims, the revolutionary new silver cars appeared, with full-width streamlined bodies (which were permissible in Formula One in those days). They caused a sensation, and no-one was surprised when Fangio won from pole position, he and team-mate Karl Kling lapping the whole field.

Over the next 15 months, until Mercedes' withdrawal in the wake of the Le Mans disaster, Fangio spearheaded their almost total domination. He was joined for their second season by Stirling

**Above:** In July 1954, after an absence of fourteen years, the mighty Mercedes-Benz concern made its return to Grand Prix racing at Reims after an absence of fourteen years with three of its fabulous 2½ litre straight-eight streamliners. Hans Herrmann retired but the incomparable Juan Manuel Fangio and team-mate Karl Kling decimated the opposition with Fangio finishing 0.1 sec ahead of the German and at least a lap ahead of the rest.

Moss as his No 2, and Moss pipped him on the finish line to win the British Grand Prix at Aintree - although Stirling doesn't really know to this day whether his team-leader let him win on that occasion.

In Fangio's own home Grand Prix on the Buenos Aires Autodromo in 1955, his extraordinary stamina came to the fore. The race was run in a freakish heat wave in the height of the Argentinian summer, and lasted - as Grands Prix did in those days - three hours. Drivers were passing out with heat exhaustion, and most cars needed two or more changes of driver to get to the finish. But Fangio swept on impassively

through the waves of stifling heat to win. Afterwards he said he'd kept going by telling himself that the sweat coursing down his body was water from a cool mountain stream.

Fangio's quiet shrewdness extended to his business dealings. He only liked to sign one-year contracts with any team he drove for, to keep his options open for the future. That, and the fact that he was always in demand as the best driver in the world, meant he could usually ensure he drove for the strongest team. In particular he was canny in his dealings with Enzo Ferrari, and he spent only one season with him, 1956 - during which he won the Championship again.

**Below**: In 1955 the Mercedes-Benz W196s of Fangio and Moss spent most of the season like this, at the head of the field. In the British Grand Prix at Aintree, however, Moss went ahead to win by 0.2 sec - and was never sure whether Fangio had let him win on his home soil.

His fifth title came in 1957, for Maserati. Now 46 years old, Fangio was motor racing's senior statesman, treated everywhere with admiration and respect. But the fire still burned fiercely. His final victory at that most testing of circuits, the old Nürburgring, was perhaps his greatest of all, when he vanquished drivers half his age in a drive of ferocious brilliance. He decided that the way to beat the Ferraris of Hawthorn and Collins was to start on half-tanks and build up enough cushion for a mid-race pitstop. By half distance he'd extended a comfortable lead, but his pitstop was a disaster: one of the knock-off wheel nuts rolled away out of sight and, as a mechanic fumbled for it under the car, the Ferraris roared by and disappeared into the distance.

After a 52-seconds stop Fangio set off in pursuit, and settled down for the drive of his life. Carving chunks off the lap record, he made up three-quarters of a minute on the Ferraris, and went by them both to win by just over three seconds. Not only had he left the old circuit record in ribbons: he'd actually lapped *7.4 seconds faster* than his own pole position the day before. Afterwards, the normally undemonstrative Fangio said he'd never driven so hard in his life, and he hoped he'd never have to again.

And he didn't. In the last two races of that season, his fifth title already secure, he finished second to the Vanwall of Stirling Moss. In 1958 he did only his home Grand Prix and one other before climbing out of the cockpit for good. The last race was at Reims, and in an ill-handling car he finished fourth. And here's a measure of the

respect for Fangio from his fellow drivers: Mike Hawthorn, leading comfortably, slowed down in the closing stages so the Great Man would not suffer the indignity of being lapped.

More than anyone, Fangio represented the sporting ethic of a period of motor racing that is now long past. He was an artist in the cockpit, tremendously fast and a daunting competitor: but he wasn't flamboyant. He didn't play to the gallery. He always said the best way to win a race was by going as slowly as possible. But if in order to win he had to go faster than anyone had ever gone before, he always seemed to be able to do it. And, as his former team-mate and life-long admirer Stirling Moss points out, you never heard anything bad about him, and from his fellow drivers you never heard anything but admiration and respect.

Out of the car he was calm and courteous, a unique blend of charm, humility, and tough acumen. And, beneath the calmness there was strong emotion. When his countryman and protégé Onofre Marimon was killed in practice at the Nürburgring he wept openly. Then, of course, he went out and won the race.

**Above**: His greatest race. In the elegant Maserati 250F, Fangio came from behind after a long pitstop to win his final victory in the 1957 German Grand Prix, shattering the Nürburgring lap record as he did so.

"FANGIO WAS AN ARTIST IN THE COCKPIT, TREMENDOUSLY FAST AND A DAUNTING COMPETITOR."

# Alberto
# ASCARI

## 1950-1955 IN HIS FATHER'S WHEELTRACKS

### MURRAY'S NOTES

• *The man who first built the Ferrari legend, winning 13 races out of 16 over a 25-month period 1951-53*

• *A glamorous cockpit stylist in those drab early post-war years, who was a specialist at winning from the front*

• *Driven by his dead father's memory. His career never recovered from leaving Ferrari for Lancia in 1954*

### FACTS

**Born:** Milan, Italy, 13 July 1918
**Died:** Monza, Italy, 26 May 1955
**Grands Prix:** 31
**First Grand Prix:** Monte Carlo 1950, Ferrari
**Last Grand Prix:** Monte Carlo 1955, Lancia
**Wins:** 13
**Pole positions:** 14
**Points:** 140.64
**Points per start:** 4.54
**Percentage wins:** 42%
**World Champion:** 1952, Ferrari; 1953, Ferrari

From the Belgian Grand Prix in June 1952 to the Belgian Grand Prix in June 1953, every single World Championship round was won by the same man in the same type of car. It was a period of domination by one driver never seen before or since - in a modern context, almost like Michael Schumacher winning 18 races on the trot. The car was the fast, sturdy four-cylinder Ferrari 500, and the man was Alberto Ascari.

In many ways Italy is the country at the historical heart of motor racing. So it comes as a shock to realise that, while Michele Alboreto (1985) and Riccardo Patrese (1992) have filled the runner-up spot, and Castellotti, Musso and De Angelis all managed third in the table, no Italian has been World Champion since Ascari's two titles in 1952 and 1953. In fact, it was this plump, dapper man from Milan who was really responsible in the first place for building Ferrari's towering and enduring reputation as the most magical of all Formula One names.

Ascari came to epitomise the strength of Italy in motor sport, with his warm personality, his blue short-sleeved shirt and cotton trousers, and his trademark blue pudding-basin crash helmet. In fact, at a time when Britain dominated the two-wheeled racing world with Norton, AJS and Velocette, so Italy did the same in the four-wheeled world with Ferrari, Maserati and Alfa-Romeo, and Alberto Ascari stood as a symbol of that domination.

He was the son of one of the great Italian motor-racing heroes of the 1920s, Antonio Ascari. Now, I know what it's like to have a famous motor-sporting father, but I can't imagine what the effect must have been on the seven-year-old Alberto when his father was killed, leading the 1925 French Grand Prix in the rain. Perhaps Jacques Villeneuve may know. But one can speculate that it was the memory of his father that drove on Alberto Ascari to be the most successful driver of his day.

His strategy was always to win from the front, and in seven of his 13 Grand Prix victories he led from start to finish. At races he was cheerful and relaxed, and never seemed to be affected by pressure - although some said that he was not at his best when he had to fight through from behind. His chunky build belied his fitness and great stamina: as with Fangio, this showed in the heat of the annual Argentine round, and in 1953, in intense heat, he started from pole, led as usual from start to finish, set fastest lap, and lapped the entire field including his own Ferrari team-mates.

I never met Ascari, but I watched him race the red Ferraris at Silverstone in 1951, 1952 and 1953. That 1951 British Grand Prix was a turning

**Right:** Alberto Ascari with the spoils of yet another victory, at Silverstone in 1953. He scored his 13 Grand Prix wins in the space of 16 races.

"BY 1949 ASCARI WAS BACK WITH FERRARI, WHICH BECAME HIS SPIRITUAL HOME."

point in F1's history, for it was the first time the screaming supercharged Alfa Romeo 159s were beaten by the big, but less thirsty, 4.5-litre Ferraris. But the man who did it wasn't Ascari: his gearbox broke. The man who pushed Fangio's Alfa down to second place was fellow-Argentinian Froilan Gonzalez, who was inspired that day.

However, the 1952 and 1953 Silverstone races were business as usual for Ascari. In an unforgettable demonstration of superiority, the blue helmeted super-star in the red car led both races from start to finish, and set fastest lap. The first of those two victories was in the absence of Fangio, who was convalescing after his Monza crash; but in 1953 Fangio was there, driving the perhaps less fleet A6GCM Maserati, and finished second a minute in arrears after almost three hours' racing.

Ascari started racing Bianchi motorcycles as a teenager. Enzo Ferrari had been his father Antonio's team-mate at Alfa Romeo 20 years before, and watched the young Alberto's progress with interest. When Ferrari ran his first car, the Tipo 815, in its first race, the 1940 Mille Miglia, he called on Ascari to drive it. It was the 22-year-old's first four-wheeled event. Once the war was over he went on to campaign Cisitalias and Maseratis with success, receiving unstinted support and guidance from his friend and mentor, Gigi Villoresi.

By 1949 he was back with Ferrari, which became his spiritual home. He won that year's Swiss Grand Prix, scoring Ferrari's first major F1 win, and the Italian Grand Prix too. When the World Championship was inaugurated the following year he was the team's lead driver. In 1951, while Gonzalez was the first to beat the Alfas at Silverstone, Ascari did it in the next two rounds, at the Nürburgring and Monza.

In 1952 and 1953 came that tremendous run of victories, and in 1952 Alberto achieved something else that was only ever emulated by Jim Clark - he scored maximum points in the championship. In those days you scored eight points for a win and one for fastest lap, but you were only allowed to count your best four scores out of the seven rounds. So his 36 points represented 100 per cent of what was possible. And, as well as heading Enzo's F1 effort for four years, he also raced his sports cars with distinction, and even tried his hand at Indianapolis, in a 4.5-litre Ferrari of course.

But after all that dominating success and those two world titles, Ferrari lost him. Enzo never paid anyone more than he could help, even a World Champion, and now Lancia were planning to enter Formula 1 for 1954. They were able to lure Ascari away from Maranello with a highly lucrative offer. As a career move, it was a disaster. Most of the 1954 season was wasted because Lancia's new D50 F1 car, with its distinctive side pannier fuel tanks, wasn't ready. By 1955 it was competitive at last. Ascari won non-championship races in Turin and Naples, and led the first two rounds in Buenos Aires and Monaco before crashing each time, spectacularly in Monte Carlo when his car somersaulted into the harbour. It looked a dreadful accident, and there was a collective sigh of relief when the blue crash helmet bobbed to the surface and Alberto struck out strongly for the nearest boat.

He spent a day in hospital having his cuts and bruises seen to, and then Lancia sent a chauffeur-driven car to take him home to Italy. On the Thursday he and Villoresi went to Monza to watch unofficial practice for the weekend's Supercortemaggiore sports car race. Ascari asked to do a few laps in Eugenio Castellotti's new, still unpainted Ferrari, and borrowed Castellotti's white helmet - which surprised Villoresi, because the deeply superstitious Ascari had always refused to drive a racing car without wearing his own blue helmet. On his third lap, the watching group in the pits suddenly heard the Ferrari's engine note fall and go silent around the back of the circuit. For no apparent reason the Ferrari had crashed at the Curva Vialone, and turned over. Ascari was thrown out and killed.

Like his father, he left a widow and two children; like his father, he was just 37 years old. And, like his father, he would surely have won more great victories had he lived.

# Stirling *MOSS*

**1952-1962** The First True Professional

If I hadn't been me, I'd have liked to have been Stirling Moss! He is of my time and he's my countryman, and as far as I'm concerned he's not only the greatest British racing driver ever. He's also the most versatile racing driver of all time.

But more than that, he's a patriot, an honest man and a true sportsman. Hale, hearty and hugely energetic in his seventies, he's still racing and rallying the sort of cars he made famous when they were new. When you remember how many other British drivers of his era died young - Hawthorn, Collins, Bristow, Stacey, Scott-Brown, Wharton, Bueb, Lewis-Evans and too many more - it's our great good fortune that he's still with us.

And he so nearly wasn't. On Easter Monday 1962 he had that dreadful accident at Goodwood that put him in a coma for weeks, and almost killed him. It ended his professional racing career. But it's extraordinary to think that, even though he hasn't been a Formula One driver for almost 40 years, his name is still a household word. Even now, in the 21st century, if you carve up a London taxi and incur the wrath of the cabbie it'll be, not Nigel Mansell, not Damon Hill, but: "Who d'you think you are? Stirling Moss?"

Yet, for today's enthusiasts, Stirling Moss has been part of the scene for so long that I don't think many of them realise what a giant superstar he was. At a time when motor racing was not of major national interest, his every move on and off the track was front-page news. Every schoolboy knows he is the greatest driver never to have won the World Championship - he finished second four years running - but few know that he took part in an incredible 496 races. He finished in 366,

and of those, even more incredibly, he won 222, which is over 60 per cent.

More than 50 of his wins were in Formula One - there were a lot of non-championship F1 races back then - but Stirling would race anything and everything: sports cars, GTs, touring cars, F2, F3 and *formule libre*. At the big meetings he'd turn out in five or six races, in different cars. One measure of his prolific success is the BRDC Gold Star, effectively an all-formula World Championship awarded on points across all classes of international racing. Stirling won it ten times. He even found time to try rallying, and became one of the few people ever to win a Coupe d'Or for completing the gruelling Alpine Rally three years running without losing a single point.

And, wherever he was in a race, whether fighting for the lead or way down the field, whatever the odds, he would always give it everything, dig deep, 110 per cent. That's why the crowds loved him. It's significant that when he had that Goodwood accident he'd lost many

**Right:** Stirling Moss with the spoils of yet another victory, after winning the Grand Prix-length Silver City Trophy at Brands Hatch in 1961, his last full season.

"THE CALM, EASY STYLE IN THE COCKPIT WAS UNMISTAKABLE: WHITE-HELMETED HEAD WELL BACK, ARMS OUTSTRETCHED, THE QUICK WAVE WHENEVER HE OVERTOOK ANYONE."

laps in a pitstop to cope with a throttle linkage problem, and was running at the back of the field with no hope of victory in what was not a major F1 event. But he wanted to give the crowd its money's worth, and was going for the lap record.

I first watched Stirling race in his early days in the late 1940s, in the little 500cc F3 Coopers. The second four-wheeled radio commentary I ever did was at the 1949 Isle of Man races. In the Manx Cup, which was effectively for 2-litre Formula Two cars, the 19-year-old Moss cheekily entered his F3 Cooper, fitted with an 1100cc V-twin JAP engine and a long-range fuel tank strapped on the side. To everyone's astonishment, including my own, he took pole position, and went on to lead the race from a V12 Ferrari and a works HWM until the magneto drive sheared with three laps to go.

Throughout the 1950s I watched his Formula One career in Maserati 250F, Mercedes-Benz, BRM, Vanwall, Cooper and Lotus. The calm, easy

style in the cockpit was always unmistakable: white-helmeted head well back, arms outstretched, the quick wave whenever he overtook anyone - in courtesy to a back-marker who'd moved aside, in impudent irony to a front-runner who'd been desperately trying to hold him off.

Alfred Neubauer of Mercedes had his eye on him, particularly after a wet qualifying session before the 1954 Swiss Grand Prix when his private Maserati was faster than everyone, Fangio included. So for 1955 Stirling was hired as No 2 to Fangio at Mercedes. He followed loyally in the great man's wheeltracks in Grands Prix, and says today he benefited hugely from the experience. He led him over the line to win the British Grand Prix at Aintree. And in the closely related 3-litre Mercedes sports car he was clearly faster than Fangio over long distances, scoring one of his greatest victories in the classic Mille Miglia with *Motor Sport* journalist Denis Jenkinson by his side.

Moss averaged almost 98 miles an hour on a thousand miles of Italian public roads, setting a record for the event that was never beaten.

In 1958, driving the Vanwall, he won more Grands Prix that anyone else, but Mike Hawthorn's consistent points-scoring with the reliable Ferrari beat him to the title by just one point. There was a move to disqualify Hawthorn from second place in the Portuguese Grand Prix because, after a spin, he'd regained the track by push-starting his car against the traffic. But Moss spoke out in his favour, saying he'd seen the incident and maintaining that Hawthorn was merely trying to get his car out of a dangerous spot. So Hawthorn got his points back - and Moss lost his chance of being Britain's first World Champion. Such sportsmanship is typical of the man, then and now, and somehow I can't see a similar situation arising in Formula One today!

Some consolation for the patriot Moss that year came in Vanwall's victory in the Constructors' Championship, which was being held for the first time that season. The British Racing Green team beat the red of Ferrari by eight points - thanks to Stirling's efforts and those of team-mate Tony Brooks.

Like Senna and Schumacher in their eras, Moss was generally accepted - once Fangio had

**Far left**: Historic victory. Stirling's win at Aintree in 1955 was the first time a Briton had won his home Grand Prix, and the first Grand Prix win of his career. He had out-qualified team-mate Fangio to take pole, too, and set fastest lap in the race.

**Below**: When Mercedes-Benz withdrew from Grand Prix racing in 1955 after two seasons of total domination, Stirling returned to Maserati. The 250F was, in my opinion, one of the most beautiful racing cars of all time and Stirling drove it to victory at Monaco and Monza with his usual stylish precision. Here, in the Belgian GP at Spa, he finished third behind the Ferraris of Peter Collins and Paul Frère.

retired - as the best driver in the world. But his dogged patriotism drove him to race British cars whenever possible, at a time when British cars weren't usually winners, and that probably kept him from being World Champion several times. Although he could have had his pick of the works teams, he spent his last three F1 seasons driving for that great private entrant, Rob Walker, with whom he scored seven of his 16 Grand Prix victories.

In his own mind, the greatest of these was Monaco in 1961. The works shark-nose Ferraris were easily the class of the field, but Moss put his old four-cylinder Lotus on pole. After three hours of racing, he led the three Ferraris over the line by just 3.7 secs. He'd had to drive at ten-tenths every inch of the way, and the official results confirmed that. His race time for the 100-lap race was precisely 40 seconds more than one hundred times his pole position time. In other words, including the standing start and coping with all the back markers, his average lap time for the

Below: In the final round of the 1958 Championship, the Moroccan Grand Prix in Casablanca, Moss led from start to finish in the Vanwall and set fastest lap - but it wasn't quite enough. Hawthorn, over 1½ minutes behind, still won the title by a single point.

whole race was only 0.4 sec off his pole time. Unbelievable!

His sports car races were hugely impressive, too. As well as that Mille Miglia victory, he won the Tourist Trophy an extraordinary seven times, plus the Targa Florio, the Nürburgring 1000 Kms, the British Empire Trophy, the Reims 12 Hours and many more. One

of his finest sports car drives was in the 1959 Tourist Trophy at Goodwood. It was the deciding round of the World Sports Car Championship, which Ferrari were set to win again, but Moss was determined to stop them in his Aston Martin. He built up a big lead in the first 80 minutes of the race, and then came in to refuel and hand over to co-driver Roy Salvadori. When Salvadori returned to hand back to Moss, fuel was spilt on a hot exhaust car and there was an immense fire. The car was destroyed, Salvadori was burned on the hand, and Moss' race seemed to be over.

But team manager John Wyer brought in the slower Shelby/Fairman Aston and put Moss into that, with instructions to go flat out. It was just the sort of challenge Moss revelled in. Shortly after half distance he had the second Aston back in the lead, and he went on to win by half a minute having driven for 4 hrs 36 mins of the six-hour race. That drive clinched the championship for Aston Martin.

In so many ways, Stirling Moss was perhaps the first truly professional racing driver. He's one of my all-time heroes not just because of his great motor-racing achievements, but also because of his patriotism, and because I know from our long friendship that he's a down-to-earth nice bloke. He's completely unspoiled: there's no side to Stirling.

His Mayfair house is famous. He designed it himself and it's full of the sort of gadgets he loves - like a carbon-fibre lift designed by Patrick Head, a self-playing grand piano, a remote-control system to run his bath to the required depth and temperature, and a dining table that descends electrically, fully laid and laden with food, through the kitchen floor into the dining room below. And, like most top drivers today, Stirling likes to do the

best deal in everything - even if it's just buying a shirt. I was doing an event with him once in Singapore, and mentioned that I'd found a brilliant Chinese tailor who'd made me several excellent shirts in a few hours. Stirling, always a snappy dresser, was immediately interested. "Do they have double-cuffs? Will he do hidden buttons? Are the collars three-ply?" In the face of this barrage of technical questions I had to admit ignorance. "How much are they?" I proudly replied that he'd only charged me £20 each. "Did you haggle? No? Wrong attitude, boy. I've got an Indian chap in London, his seams are brilliant, he does the buttons how I want them, and I pay him £14."

Brisk, incisive, personable, eloquent and considerate, he's eternally cheerful and positive, he's universally popular, and his professionalism and limitless energy mean he's made a brilliant job of exploiting his image and reputation ever since his racing career ended. He's also a fine broadcaster, with a lot of TV and radio work under his belt. And in Susie he's got the most charming wife who is as professional as he is in organising his still hectic life.

Stirling Moss is a national institution. It took the powers-that-be four decades to comprehend that fully, but finally, in the Millennium Honours List, Stirling was created a Knight of the Realm and became Sir Stirling. For what he has done for his country on the worldwide motor racing stage, it is nothing more than he richly deserved.

**Above**: For his last three seasons Moss was faithful to Rob Walker's privateer team, in whose blue colours with white noseband he won seven Grands Prix. Here he accelerates out of the Station Hairpin at Monaco in the Lotus 18 en route to victory in 1961.

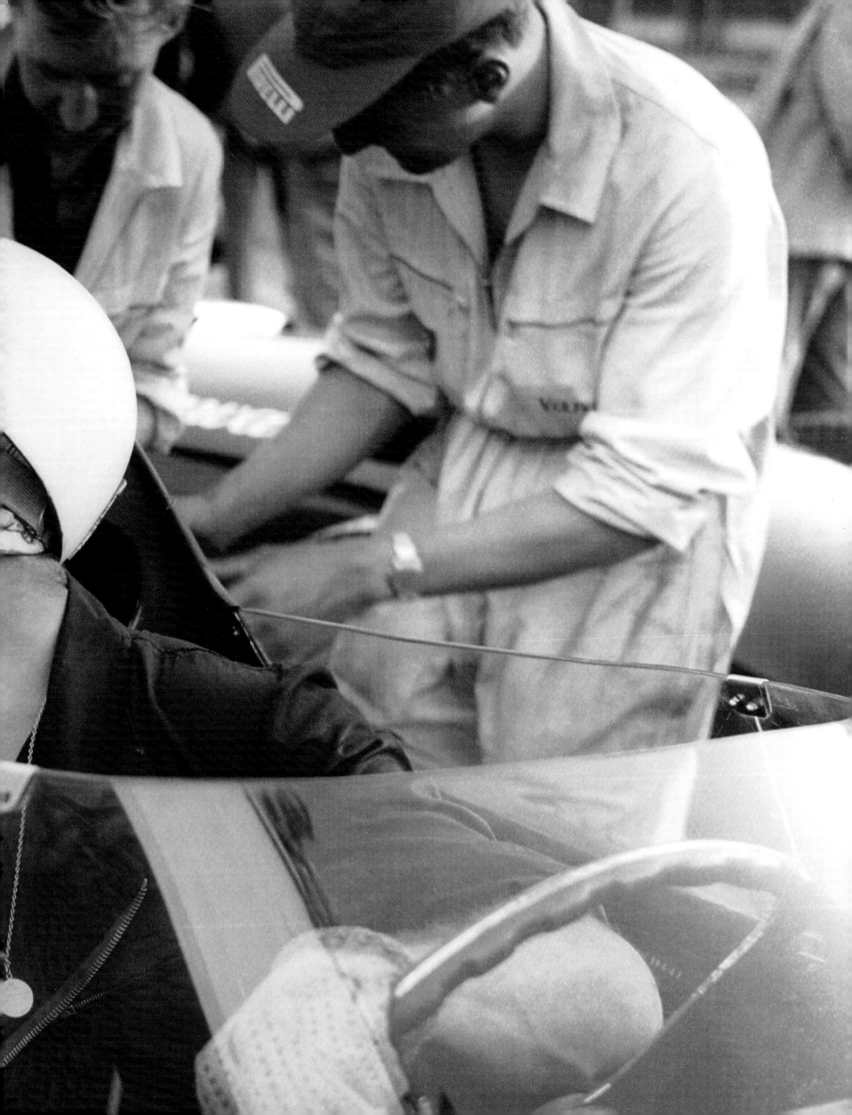

# Jack
# BRABHAM

**1955-1970** THE QUIET AUSTRALIAN

There's only one man in the history books who won the World Championship in a car with his own name on the nose. That man is Sir Jack Brabham, who won the title three times, and in the first 30 years of the World Championship was the only man apart from Fangio to be champion more than twice. His F1 career spanned three decades: he started in the laid-back days of the 1950s, and won his last victory as sponsorship and professionalism took off in the 1970s.

Jack was the first of the Commonwealth champions, to be followed by Denny Hulme, Jody Scheckter and Alan Jones. Like his Commonwealth motorcycling counterparts such as Harry Hinton, Jim Redman, Tom Phillis, Ray Amm, Bob Brown and Ken Kavanagh, Jack had the courage and the initiative to leave home and go to Europe, and the talent to conquer the world.

He grew up in the tough nursery of Australian dirt-track racing, which left him with a spectacular tail-out driving style. On the track he asked no quarter and certainly gave none - ask anyone who raced against him! He arrived in Britain in 1955 and gravitated straight towards the Cooper factory, where he appointed himself unpaid dogsbody and van driver. And he managed to wangle an entry in the British Grand Prix at Aintree that year in a Bristol-powered bobtail Cooper sports car. Soon John and Charles Cooper realised that this taciturn young man was not only an aggressive and press-on racer but also a hugely inspired engineer, of the classic Australian practical, no-nonsense school. They let him build up his own Formula Two Cooper in a corner of the shop, and by the time Cooper were ready to

move into Formula One in 1957 Jack was their No 1 works driver.

In 1958 Stirling Moss made history by scoring the first Formula One victory for a rear-engined car, but that was in Rob Walker's own Cooper. It was at Monaco in 1959 that Jack scored his and the Cooper works team's first win. He took the championship that year, and Cooper the constructors' title, and 1960 was a repeat performance. A front-engined car would never win the World Championship again. His pioneering spirit, and John Cooper's, also sowed the seeds of a separate rear-engined revolution at the hallowed Indianapolis Speedway, when he drove a specially adapted four-pot Cooper-Climax in the 1961 500 and finished ninth.

More perhaps than any other World Champion, Jack Brabham liked to be his own mechanic. Not for him the social round, and he disliked the prizegivings and the parties. He preferred to be in the garage, preparing his own car his way. He always built up his own car himself at the start of each season, and his

**Right**: In the entire 50-year history of Formula One only two men have won more World Championships than Jack Brabham - Juan Manuel Fangio and Alain Prost.

**Above**: Brabham at Zandvoort in 1966 with the most successful car of the new three-litre formula, the V8 Brabham-Repco BT19. This was one of Jack's four wins on the trot which clinched his third title.

comments that he must be past it by appearing on the starting grid at Zandvoort with walking stick and long grey beard - and then winning the race. In fact he won four brilliant Grand Prix victories on the trot that year, which was more than enough to clinch his third World title and, of course, the Constructors' Championship.

The following year the Brabham team was on top again, but this time Jack was runner-up in the championship to his team-mate, New Zealander Denny Hulme. Jack

development skills helped the cars grow steadily in competitiveness. Certainly, his role in Cooper's tremendous success in the late 1950s goes far beyond just the driving.

Not surprisingly, therefore, he soon decided he should be his own boss. At the end of 1961 he left Cooper, and eight months later the first Brabham F1 car made its debut in the German Grand Prix. It had been designed by his old friend Ron Tauranac, a fellow Aussie whom Jack had persuaded to come to England to be his partner. In its third race, the Mexican Grand Prix, Jack finished second, and the marque was on its way.

Come 1966 and the advent of the new 3-litre formula, the Australian connection was reinforced when Jack used the light, simple V8 Repco engine in his new BT19. It wasn't the most powerful engine on the grid, but it was torquey and reliable, and unlike some of its competitors it was ready for the start of the season. Jack was now the wrong side of 40, famously responding to press

continued racing until he was nearly 45, and in his final season in 1970 he won the opening round at Kyalami and came so close to winning two more, famously crashing on the final corner of the Monaco Grand Prix under pressure from Rindt, and then running out of fuel at the very end of the British round at Brands Hatch. He qualified on the second row for his final Grand Prix in Mexico City, only to drop out with low oil pressure. Then at last he did retire, to concentrate on a multitude of shrewd and successful business ventures in Australia and Britain. But the Brabham name lived on in motor sport, not only because Bernie Ecclestone bought the team and took it to two more World Championships, but because Jack's three sons, Geoff, Gary and David, all went on to distinguish themselves in the cockpit.

Jack himself found it difficult to keep away, too. I watched him driving as hard and as aggressively as ever, aged 73, in the 1999 Goodwood Revival. In streaming wet conditions, on a track on which he'd been a winner 40 years before, he raced a fearsome Cobra (until it lost a wheel), then a Cooper-Climax like the ones that brought him his first two championships, and finally a McLaren-BRM from the era of his third title. It was in this, duelling on the limit with Jackie Oliver's Lotus 49, that he went off in a

has been hard of hearing. But everything he says is very much worth listening to, and his stories of his racing career, told with economy and self-deprecating wit, are a joy. I was lucky enough to join him and Lady Brabham at Lord March's Goodwood Revival meeting dinner party, along with Tony Brooks, Dan Gurney and Phil Hill,

big way and hit the bank. It was a frightening accident, and he was lucky to escape with three cracked three ribs and a damaged vertebra. Within days he was out and about again, and already talking about what he'd drive in the next Goodwood Revival.

Jack is still a quiet man, and for some years

and that was an experience to cherish. From his humble beginnings around the speedway tracks of New South Wales to be thrice World Champion, for a while the world's biggest manufacturer of single-seater racing cars, and Australia's first motor racing knight, Sir Jack Brabham's life has been one of truly heroic achievement.

**Above:** Just before his 44th birthday, Brabham scored his final Grand Prix win in the South African GP at Kyalami. The car is the Cosworth-powered BT33.

# Phil
# HILL

## MURRAY'S NOTES

• *Sensitive, intellectual, deep-thinking driver: a contrast to previous champions, and the first North American to take the title*

• *A sports car driver who translated into Formula One*

• *His F1 career collapsed when he left Ferrari, although he plugged on with lesser teams*

## FACTS

**Born**: Miami, USA, 20 April 1927
**Grands Prix**: 48
**First Grand Prix**: Reims 1958, Bonnier Maserati
**Last Grand Prix**: Monza 1966, Eagle
**Wins**: 3
**Pole positions**: 6
**Points**: 98
**Points per start**: 2.04
**Percentage wins**: 6%
**World Champion**: 1961, Ferrari

It was Philip T. Hill's heroic achievement to be the first American to win the World Championship. Since then there has only been one other, the Italian-born Mario Andretti. Phil won just three World Championship Grands Prix, but he was always very quick. In his championship year he started from pole position in all but two of the rounds that Ferrari entered. But when he clinched the title by winning the Italian Grand Prix at Monza, there were no celebrations. Tragically his team-mate Wolfgang von Trips, the debonair German count, had been killed in the opening stages of the race, along with 13 spectators.

Phil came to Formula One by way of sports car racing. He started in minor events on the USA's West Coast, first in humbler cars he'd saved up to buy himself, then in Ferraris entered by wealthy privateers. His successes for Luigi Chinetti's North American Racing Team brought him to Enzo Ferrari's attention and he was invited to join the works sports car team, arriving in Europe for the 1956 Nürburgring 1000Kms to find himself, to his amazement, part of a line-up that included Fangio, Collins, Castellotti, Musso, de Portago and Gendebien. The latter became his usual co-driver, and the pairing twice won the Le Mans 24 Hours.

At that time Ferrari treated sports car racing just as seriously as Formula One, and it wasn't until the 1958 Italian Grand Prix at Monza that Enzo offered him a pukka F1 drive. On Ferrari's home turf he set fastest race lap and finished third - an extraordinary achievement for an F1 rookie - and in his next race, the final round in

Morocco, he was lying second when he eased off to let Mike Hawthorn past so the Englishman could clinch the World Championship. He'd shown what he could do, and from then on he was a fully fledged F1 team member.

By now the front-engined Ferraris were being overshadowed by the nimble little rear-engined Coopers, particularly on the twistier circuits, but he won the 1960 Italian Grand Prix and set fastest lap. Then for 1961 Ferrari's own rear-engined car was ready, and it proved to be almost unbeatable. The Scuderia arrived at Monza for the penultimate round with von Trips leading the championship on 33 points and Hill second on 29. Two laps into the race von Trips was dead. Phil, not knowing what had happened, won the race, only to learn the grim news after he'd taken the flag.

In 1962, as reigning champion, he found Ferrari completely eclipsed by the new-generation Lotuses and BRMs, although he did manage a second and two thirds. At the end of the season, along with much of the team's management, he fell out with the Commendatore and joined Carlo Chiti's breakaway ATS outfit. That was a complete

disaster, and after an indifferent 1964 with Cooper his F1 career petered out. However, he continued to shine in long-distance sports car racing as a member of the American Chaparral team.

Deep-thinking, intense and highly intelligent, Phil was in marked contrast to the extrovert Grand Prix drivers of his era. In retirement he built up one of the best classic car restoration businesses in the world, expanded his remarkable collection of recorded classical music, and - like Moss, Stewart, Hunt and others - became a successful TV commentator.

I never met him when he was racing, but have had the privilege of knowing him as a friend for many years. Today he is friendly, approachable, and a brilliant conversationalist. His analytical brain and sharp wit make his I-was-there slants on motor-racing in the 1950s and 1960s wonderful to hear. Few drivers spent more of their career inside the Ferrari works team, and his memories of Maranello are magical stuff.

He is another who still races historic cars, and meanwhile his son Derek is now making his way up the motor-racing ladder. One of the highlights of the 1999 Goodwood Revival meeting was watching Phil and Derek share one of the mighty Daytona Cobras, bringing it into a magnificent second place in the rain-soaked TT celebration. Phil is another great driver who survived an era when so many of his colleagues were killed, and it is our good fortune that he's with us still to tell us so eloquently how it was back then.

"FEW DRIVERS SPENT MORE OF THEIR CAREER INSIDE THE FERRARI WORKS TEAM, AND HILL'S MEMORIES OF MARANELLO ARE MAGICAL STUFF."

# Jim CLARK

**1960-1968** SHEER NATURAL GENIUS

One of the few regrets of my motor-racing life is that I never met Jim Clark. During his great years I was almost totally involved in commentating on other types of wheeled sport, and in 1968, when he was at the height of his career, came the tragic waste of his death in a minor Formula Two race in Germany. So for me he is a hero by repute - and none the less for that, because clearly he was head and shoulders above everyone else in his own time, just as Fangio, Moss, Senna and Schumacher were in theirs.

When you talk of Jim Clark, you talk of natural ability. This man was a shy Scottish sheep farmer who had no ambition at all to be in the limelight, or to be rich and famous. He just enjoyed driving cars as fast as they could be made to go, and almost without effort he found he was better at it than anyone else. His early efforts in Scottish club racing were just something to do on his weekends off from the farm. Then he met Colin Chapman.

Chapman, who as you'll see on another page was one of my non-driving heroes, was the most brilliant racing car designer of his time. He'd founded Lotus and built it up from a part-time business in a shed to a fast-growing sports car firm, and in character he was about as different from Jimmy as it was possible to be - a fast-talking hustler, decisive, driven, fiercely ambitious. They made an unlikely pair, but their working relationship became one of the most successful in motor racing history.

Jim was the son of a prosperous Scottish farmer, and left public school at 16 to work on one of the family farms near Duns, in

Berwickshire. The pull of that farm was to remain a conflict within him throughout his racing career. He'd been driving tractors since he was tiny, and around the farm drove first the family Austin 7 and then his father's Alvis. So as soon as he was 17 there were local rallies, and then club races in his friend Ian Scott-Watson's DKW and Porsche. The Scottish team, Border Reivers, noticed his talent and put him in a D-type Jaguar and an old Lister-Jaguar, and he chalked up a string of wins and lap records. So for 1959 the Reivers' patron, Jock McBain, thought about a Formula Two car for his young protégé and arranged for him to try a Lotus 16 at Brands Hatch.

Colin Chapman was astonished by Clark's speed even before he was told that the Scot had never driven a single-seater before, and never been round Brands Hatch. Chapman, ever the dealer, sold Scott-Watson an Elite that day - and then at the Boxing Day Brands Hatch meeting soon afterwards the Lotus boss found Clark was quicker in Scott-Watson's customer car than he was in the works car!

**Right**: Jimmy Clark hated Spa, yet he won the Belgian Grand Prix on this frighteningly fast road circuit four years running. After his 1962 win, his eyes betray the strain.

Several teams had noticed this young man's talent and other offers started to come in, but Chapman was determined to hang onto him. For 1960 Lotus signed Clark for Formula Junior and Formula 2, while he continued to drive for Border Reivers in sports car races (he was third at Le Mans that year in their Aston Martin). By June Chapman put him in an F1 Lotus 18 for the Dutch Grand Prix, and in half a dozen GPs that first year Jimmy was in the points three times and on the podium once - at a time when Lotuses rarely finished races, and never looked like beating the might of Ferrari, or the light simplicity of Cooper.

**Above:** Great driver. Great car. Great engine. When Colin Chapman persuaded Walter Hayes of Ford to authorise an investment of £100,000 in Cosworth to produce the DFV V8, he sowed the seeds of a brilliant partnership. In 1967, with the great Jim Clark at the wheel, the legendary Lotus 49 won first time out in Holland and again in Britain, America and Mexico. This is Clark trying a new visor in practice at Monza.

A special chemistry had rapidly developed between Chapman and Clark, and Jimmy was to remain the star of Team Lotus for the rest of his life. Every one of his 72 Grands Prix was at the wheel of a works Lotus, and every one of the 25 Lotus victories between 1962 and his death was scored by him. For 1961 Formula One was changed from 2.5-litres to 1.5-litres, but with simple four-pot Climax power Jimmy did well to get thirds at Zandvoort and Reims. Then in 1962 Lotus had the Climax V8 and Clark fought a season-long battle with Graham Hill's V8 BRM for the championship, which was only resolved by Jimmy's car springing an oil leak when he was leading the final round in South Africa.

No such problems in 1963: Clark simply swept the board. You could only count your best six results at that time, and Clark echoed Ascari's 1952 achievement of hitting a maximum - actually he won seven of the 10 rounds, had a second place when his car developed a misfire, and a third (and fastest lap) after being left on the grid at Watkins Glen with a flat battery. Lotus had reliability problems in 1964 - there were three more wins, but seven retirements - but in 1965 he finished six of the ten races, and won every time. Another maximum score, another World title.

When the 3-litre Formula One was introduced in 1966 Lotus at first divided their effort between the little Climax V8 in 2-litre form, which was underpowered, and the heavy and complex H16 BRM unit, so this was a fallow period for Clark - except that he scored the H16's only race win in the United States Grand Prix. But by the third round of 1967 the Cosworth DFV engine made its bow in Chapman's new Lotus 49. Jimmy won first time out at Zandvoort, the first of four victories that year, giving him third in the World Championship behind the reliable Brabham-Repcos of Hulme

conquering form. His fingernails were always bitten down to the quick, and before a race his

and Brabham. In 1968, with the 49 now well sorted, Jimmy was clear favourite for the title, and started as he meant to go on by comfortably winning the opening round at Kyalami. But, tragically, it was his last victory, and his last Grand Prix.

It was never in Clark's nature to complain, or argue, or try to exert influence over the team he drove for. Chapman designed and built the cars - always clever, usually fragile, often unreliable - and Clark, unquestioningly, got in and drove them faster than anyone would have thought possible. He never seemed to work on his technique, or analyse what he was doing: he was just devastatingly fast, everywhere.

But, lest you should think that Clark's effortless speed denoted a phlegmatic nature, he clearly had to dig deep to produce that all-

face would take on a haunted, hounded look. He always hated Spa, the terrifyingly fast old circuit on public roads through the Ardennes forests. On his first visit there, at a sports car meeting, his fellow-Scot Archie Scott-Brown crashed in flames and died from his burns. The first time he went there in an F1 car his Lotus team-mate and friend Alan Stacey was killed when a bird hit him in the face at speed and, stunned, he went off the road. Yet Clark was always invincible at Spa. He scored his first Grand Prix win there, going on to win the Belgian GP four years running, and he usually set fastest lap. This was true bravery, a quiet man's unobtrusive courage.

From that first victory at Spa to his last, a few weeks before he was killed, Jimmy did 56 Grands Prix. He led 42 of them, and won 25, a remarkable record of speed and consistency.

**Above**: Clark's last Grand Prix victory - and the last time the classic pre-advertising green and yellow Team Lotus colours were seen in a Grand Prix - was at Kyalami in 1968.

**Below**: In 1963, lured by massive support from Ford and an enormous prize fund, Lotus entered the lion's den by taking on the entrenched American racing establishment at the world's most famous track, Indianapolis. Jim Clark electrified the USA by finishing second in the Indy 500, contentiously beaten by Parnelli Jones' oil-dropping Agajanian Special. The next year Clark retired from a commanding lead. In 1967 he won. Indy was conquered and its front-engined monsters were no more.

When his Lotus held together, he was usually first past the flag. He never seemed to have an off-day, and he was devastatingly fast on every type of track - from round-the-houses to high-speed road circuits to American ovals. He also demonstrated a Moss-like ability to be fast in just about anything. He won in Colin's Lotus Cortinas, made his treacherous Lotus 30 sports-racer go far faster than it should have done, raced huge Ford Galaxies and tiny Lotus 23s, and conquered the Indianapolis 500, finishing second in 1963 and then winning it in 1965 - the first non-American to do so for half a century.

By the time Jimmy was killed the Lotus/Cosworth/Ford relationship was really starting to work well, and Lotus were to win two more championships in the next three years with

Tyrrell. One of the great questions that tragedy has rendered unanswered - just like Senna versus Schumacher - is who would ultimately have had the best of a protracted battle for supremacy between Clark and Chapman, and Stewart and Tyrrell. But there isn't any doubt that, had Clark not died when he did, he would have added more World Championship titles to the two he won in 1963 and 1965.

If, that is, he had continued racing much longer. Clark coped good-humouredly with the increasing media exposure and stardom which was beginning to gather momentum in the second half of the 1960s, but it was always hard to tell what this quiet man really felt about the pressures of being the best driver in the world. Certainly you had the impression that he always left the

Graham Hill and Jochen Rindt. After Clark's death the dominating relationship in F1 was that between another Scot, Jackie Stewart, and Ken

noise and hubbub of the racetrack and returned to the Scottish hillsides with relief. And at the end of his life, when his huge earnings and his natural

Scottish frugality dictated that he should live abroad for a spell to reduce his tax bill (he based himself in Bermuda, sharing a flat in Paris with French journalist Jabby Crombac when he was in Europe), he seemed unhappy with the peripatetic life that his huge success had saddled him with.

But 1968 promised better. After his South African win - his 25th Grand Prix victory, breaking Fangio's long-standing record - he went to Australia and won the Tasman Series, and thence to Indianapolis to try the wedge-shaped Lotus turbine car that he would drive in the 500 in May. His year of tax exile was up on April 5, so as soon as he'd got a German Formula Two race at Hockenheim out of the way on April 7 he'd be able to move back to his beloved Scotland.

In fact, that first weekend in April Jimmy was to have driven the Ford F3L, the DFV-powered Alan Mann GT car, in the BOAC 500 sports car race at Brands Hatch. But at the last minute, bowing to his Lotus contract, he changed his plans to take in the F2 Hockenheim. The chicane that today slows cars down going into the Ostkurve, the right-hander at the top of the circuit, wasn't there, and it was merely a long high-speed curve cutting through the forest. That was where one of Jimmy's rear tyres apparently deflated. He went off into the trees and was killed instantly.

Like so many other British enthusiasts, I was at Brands Hatch that day for the BOAC race, and I remember how the news reached me as I walked from the car park to the grandstand. It was accompanied by a feeling of total disbelief, for it is the truly greatest drivers who always seem invincible, immortal. And Jimmy Clark belonged to that tiny band, for he set the standard for his era. He will always be one of my heroes.

**Above**: In the elegant monocoque Lotus 25 and its successor, the 33, the little 1500 cc Coventry Climax V8 found the perfect partner. Clark scored an astonishing 19 Grand Prix victories in these cars over four seasons.

# Dan GURNEY

**1959-1970** A CALM TALENT

## MURRAY'S NOTES

• *Relaxed, undemonstrative manner and quiet American charm belies a much-underrated driver of great talent*

• *Versatility: achievements in Indycar, CanAm and NASCAR even greater than in Formula One*

• *Like Brabham, raced - and finally won - in his own Grand Prix car, going on to build thriving Indycar business*

## FACTS

**Born**: Port Jefferson, USA, 13 April 1931
**Grands Prix**: 86
**First Grand Prix**: Reims 1959, Ferrari
**Last Grand Prix**: Brands Hatch 1970, McLaren
**Wins**: 4
**Points**: 133
**Points per start**: 1.54
**Percentage wins**: 5%

Like Phil Hill, Dan Gurney is an American who rose to the top of Formula One, and like Jack Brabham he's a driver who built and raced his own car. Unlike Phil he never won the World Championship, and he won just a single Grand Prix with his sleek, beautiful Eagles. But ask the great drivers of the 1960s who their top rivals were, and they'll always mention Daniel Sexton Gurney.

The other thing everyone says about Dan is how, in a working life around motor racing as a driver, constructor, entrant and team chief, he has always remained what he was when he started: a warm, calm and delightfully friendly man. When he finally won the 1967 Belgian Grand Prix in his blue and white Anglo-American Racers Eagle-Weslake V12, there can have been no more popular victory. It made him the first, and so far the only, American to win a Grand Prix in an American car since Jimmy Murphy's Duesenberg won the French GP in 1921.

Dan was born the son of an opera singer and grew up near California's Riverside Raceway. Almost too tall for a racing car cockpit, he started racing with a Triumph TR2, moved on to Porsches and Ferraris, and then followed his friend Phil Hill to the works Ferrari sports car team. Enzo gave him his Formula One chance in 1959, less than four years after his first Californian club race. Dan repaid the compliment by finishing second in his second Grand Prix, and third in his third. This was the year that the mercurial Frenchman Jean Behra lost his Ferrari drive after fisticuffs with team-manager Tavoni in the Reims pits, which helped cement Gurney's seat with the team.

But easy-going Dan wasn't enamoured of all the Ferrari politics, so he switched to BRM. The Bourne cars were dreadfully unreliable that year and he barely finished a race, so he moved on to Porsche, for two reliable but underpowered years with the German firm's short-lived F1 team. The high spot came in the French Grand Prix at Rouen in 1962, when Hill and Clark both retired and Dan led home Tony Maggs' Cooper and Ritchie Ginther's BRM to score Porsche's only Grand Prix victory as a manufacturer, ever.

Then Dan found a happy home at Brabham, where he stayed for three seasons as Jack's first team-mate in his own team. He proved every bit as fast as Jack, winning at Rouen again and in Mexico, and in his last five Grands Prix for Brabham he was on the podium every time.

But, like Jack, he longed to run his own F1 team, and the elegant and beautifully made Eagle appeared in 1966. Its Weslake V12 engine wasn't ready, so for most of its first season Dan made do with an old four-cylinder Climax. He stuck with the project for three long, frustrating years, and at last, among a string of retirements, came that great Spa victory in 1967. But, apart from a non-championship win in the Race of Champions at

Brands Hatch, that was to be an F1 one-off. At the end of 1968 he gave up the unequal struggle of running his own Grand Prix team from England.

All the while this most versatile of drivers had been equally busy in almost every other branch of the sport. In fact, I can't think of another driver who has won major victories in Formula One, USAC, NASCAR and World Championship sports car racing, all pretty much at the same time. He played a major role in initiating Colin Chapman, and Ford, into the possibilities of Indianapolis; he won Le Mans for Ford; and twice he won the Riverside 500 NASCAR race. When that other great driver/constructor Bruce McLaren was tragically killed testing at Goodwood, Gurney was drafted into the McLaren CanAm team to support Denny Hulme, and he won the first two races of the 1970 series, as well as doing three more GPs that year for Bruce's team.

Rather like Tony Brooks, Dan was always a driver for whom his own colleagues on the grid had huge respect, even if his smooth, undramatic driving style didn't play to the gallery. Jim Clark privately admitted he was the one driver whose skill he reckoned matched his own. If Dan had made it his major priority to get the best drive available to him in Formula One, he would surely have won many more Grands Prix, and possibly a World Championship.

When he retired as a driver he continued to run his Eagles in USAC (now Champcar) racing and, while his best finish at Indianapolis as a driver was second, Eagles have won the race three times. His relationship with Toyota has also brought considerable success in IMSA racing. Best of all, his friendly presence is still seen at historic events like Goodwood, where a privately-owned Eagle-Weslake has occasional outings to remind us what the prettiest of all 1960s F1 cars looked and sounded like.

**Above:** Every inch a racing car. The lovely Anglo-American Racers Gurney Eagle, with Weslake V12 engine, rounds La Source Hairpin at Spa during its finest day, when Dan won the 1967 Belgian Grand Prix.

# *John* SURTEES

**1960-1972** ON TWO WHEELS AND FOUR

Conditions at the August 1951 Thruxton motorcycle meeting were vile. I certainly wasn't expecting it to be a day to remember as, in torrential rain, I clambered nervously onto the slippery roof of the double-decker bus that was my BBC vantage point. But that was the memorable day that a virtually unknown 17-year-old called John Surtees rode his 500cc Vincent Grey Flash to an amazing second place, beaten only by the illustrious Geoff Duke.

It was the start of an unparalleled career of achievement in motor sport. To become a motorcycle World Champion is outstanding, but to do so seven times in four years is incredible. Then to become Formula One World Champion as well is absolutely unique. That is what John has done, and I still marvel at it.

If my passionate interest in motor sport is in the genes, then John's is too. His father Jack was an accomplished sidecar racer who competed against the likes of the great World Champion Eric Oliver in the heady post-war days of the late 1940s and early 50s. John passengered for him when he was only 14 - I remember racing my 250 AJS on the original Brands Hatch grass track when Jack and John were in the sidecar event - but his ambition was to race solos. Encouraged and helped by his father, he took to it like a duck to water, dedicatedly building another talent that was to serve him well: that of a meticulous and gifted engineer and tuner.

He was a racing natural, and his first victory came on the Vincent in 1950 when he was only 16. In 1952, after a brilliant run of success in national events, he changed the Grey Flash for a

500cc Manx Norton, and from then on he never looked back. He racked up 20 wins in 1953, over 60 the following year, and more than 70 in 1955 - including beating Duke on a 500cc Gilera at Silverstone in 1955. I was privileged to describe scores of them for the BBC. The man was a phenomenon. His riding style was smooth, serene and immaculate, and his bikes were always an object lesson in terms of preparation and performance. But the best was yet to come.

In 1956 Italy's Count Domenico Agusta made Surtees an offer he couldn't refuse. The fabled MV Agusta team badly needed John's unique combination of riding and development talents to overcome the dominant Gilera fours. It was an inspired move by Agusta, for that unique mix of Surtees talents rapidly transformed the team into a world-beater. In his first year for MV John became 500cc World Champion, and for the next three years he won both the 350 and 500cc championships. As he had been in British national events on the Norton, so in international Grands Prix on the MV he was virtually unbeatable. He scored 38 championship victories and a superb

**Above:** John Surtees had won almost 200 races on self-tuned Manx Nortons by the time he was 21.

six Isle of Man TT wins in just five years.

After such domination of his chosen sport, John thirsted for a new challenge. With no works opponents to conquer and not enough races to satisfy his appetite, he turned to four wheels.

Having watched his two-wheel career for so long, I naturally followed his move to racing cars with keen interest. Both Vanwall and Aston Martin had given him tests in 1959, and in the Vanwall he had been only fractionally slower

talent and, although John was still in his last year with MV, Colin Chapman wasted no time in recruiting him to drive for Lotus. In only his second Grand Prix, sandwiched by MV 500cc wins in Belgium and Germany, John was second to World Champion Jack Brabham in the 1960 British Grand Prix. It was the start of a 13-year motor racing career that was to rival his motorcycle years, and almost cost him his life.

Chapman, always excited by new driving

**Above**: Neck and neck. Surtees wins the 1967 Italian Grand Prix in the RA300 Honda V12, by a fifth of a second from Jack Brabham.

than Stirling Moss. But his actual car racing debut came in a Formula Junior Cooper in 1960, at Goodwood, where he finished second to Jim Clark's works Lotus. Not bad!

Here, clearly, was a man with enormous

talent, wanted Surtees to partner Clark in the Lotus F1 team for 1961. That would indeed have been a superteam. But John wasn't happy about the way Chapman was proposing to terminate Innes Ireland's contract to accommodate him, and

"NOT MANY PEOPLE
TURN FERRARI DOWN,
AND EVEN FEWER
GET ASKED AGAIN!"

in the end he took a step backwards and signed for the disappointing Yeoman Credit Cooper outfit, driving also in the 2.5-litre Intercontinental Formula and New Zealand Tasman races. The following year, with the new Lola F1 team, wasn't much better, but the talent was there for all to see. Whenever the car got to the end of the race, John was in the points. He was fourth at Monaco, and then a magnificent second to Jim Clark in the British Grand Prix at Aintree, and a fortnight later he was second to Graham Hill in the German round at the Nürburgring.

But, once again, Italy was about to play a major role in his career. The great Enzo Ferrari wanted John to inject new life into the Scuderia. Actually, it wasn't the first time John had been to Maranello: the previous year he'd refused a contract because of his then limited experience -

and because he hadn't been too impressed with some aspects of the Ferrari organisation. Not many people turn Ferrari down, and even fewer get asked again! But now there were special circumstances. After disagreements with Enzo, several of the team's top men - and their World Champion Phil Hill - had left to found the catastrophically unsuccessful ATS team. Ferrari, like MV seven years earlier, needed John to drive for them, and remotivate them.

They got him, and both prospered. Surtees loves Italy and the Italians, he speaks fluent Italian, and his determined and demanding leadership transformed the team. Over the next three years he won four Grands Prix for the Scuderia, including the German Grand Prix two years running, and to the hysterical delight of the *tifosi* he won the Italian Grand Prix at

Monza in 1964. Helped by second places at Zandvoort, Watkins Glen and Mexico City, that was the year that John vanquished Hill and Clark to give Ferrari both the Drivers' and Constructors' Championships.

While all this was going on there was a raft of sports car successes, too - he won the Sebring 12 Hours, the Nürburgring 1000 Kms (twice) and the Monza 1000 Kms, and was third at Le Mans. And, in a Lola T70 rather than a Ferrari, there was one dreadful accident. In practice for the 1965 CanAm race at Mosport Park in Canada a front wheel came off, with disastrous and almost fatal results. The car somersaulted over the barriers and landed on top of him, and he was hospitalised for three months. But the next year, undaunted, he returned - and won the CanAm Championship!

It has to be said that John is not the easiest man in the world to get on with. He is basically a very cheery bloke, but he is also immovably determined, enormously demanding, opinionated and dogmatic, and he expects everyone else to achieve the same stratospherically high standards

**Below**: At the end of 1968 Honda withdrew from Formula One. Their V12 was too heavy and John could only manage one second place that year, in France. Here, in the Spanish Grand Prix at Jarama, the gear linkage broke.

which he sets and achieves himself. He is very much his own man, and he does not suffer fools gladly. All this leads to confrontations, and it did at Ferrari in 1966 when, just after he had won the Belgian Grand Prix at Spa, John and the team's race director Eugenio Dragoni fell out. John walked out there and then, finishing the year with Cooper-Maserati, which won him the Mexican Grand Prix and helped him to second place in the Championship. Then he joined forces with Honda and Lola for the Japanese firm's second go at Formula One.

This two-year relationship produced one of the most dramatic finishes in the history of F1 when John beat Jack Brabham over the Monza finishing line by 0.2 sec to win the 1967 Italian Grand Prix. There were three podiums, too, including second place in the tragic French Grand Prix at Rouen. That was when Jo Schlesser was killed in the new air-cooled V8 car which John had told Honda was nowhere near ready to race. But there were no more wins, and at the end of 1968 Honda withdrew from Formula One.

Then, after a miserable season with BRM (wrong time, wrong team, wrong engine), John founded his own organisation in 1970 to race his own Surtees cars in F1 and F2. He soon found that trying to run Team Surtees to his own perfectionist standards was immensely time-consuming, and his active driving career was now coming to an end. His last F1 win came in the non-championship Oulton Park Gold Cup in

1971 - which was also the year his friend, former motorcycle rival and now Team Surtees member Mike Hailwood took the European Formula Two

Championship, and so nearly won the Italian Grand Prix.

Big John, as the Italians affectionately call him, ran in his last Grand Prix at Monza the following year. He qualified 19th, and retired after 20 laps with fuel vaporisation. He may have failed to match Jack Brabham by winning a Grand Prix in a car carrying his own name (although in that final year he took F2 Surtees cars to victory in Japan and Italy). But, praise the Lord, we certainly haven't seen the last of him. He still delights us with very rapid demonstration drives of priceless pre-war Mercedes-Benz and Auto Union Grand Prix cars, and rides at the superb Goodwood Festival of Speed and Revival meetings on magnificently restored bikes from his own mouth-watering collection. Long may he do so. They don't make 'em like John any more.

**Above:** The final Formula One victory of John's career was in his own Surtees TS7 in the 1971 Oulton Park Gold Cup.

# Mike
# HAILWOOD

## MURRAY'S NOTES

• On two wheels, a talent unprecedented and unequalled. On four, he rarely had the chance to show his mettle

• A reluctant hero, pushed by his ambitious father, and a decent, cheerful, friendly man

• Astonishing versatility on two wheels translated to four: great sports car driver, F5000 and F2

## FACTS

**Born**: Great Milton, England, 4 April 1940
**Died**: Birmingham, England, 23 March 1981
**Grands Prix**: 50
**First Grand Prix**: Silverstone 1963, Parnell Lotus
**Last Grand Prix**: Nürburgring 1974, McLaren
**Points**: 29
**Points per start**: 0.58

In all my years of passionately following motor sport, one man stands out above everyone else in my affection and regard: Mike Hailwood. Partly, I suppose, it's because I knew him so well during what was a very impressionable part of my life. But mostly it's because of his endearing personality, his fascinating background and his brilliant achievements.

But what's he doing in a book of Formula One heroes, when his legendary prowess was with motorcycles rather than with cars? Well, I'm proud to say that we were both heavily involved with the motorcycle and car Grand Prix worlds at the same time; that his impact on Formula One was considerable; and that, had he not had the misfortune to end his four-wheeled career with a heavy crash in 1974, I am convinced he could have gone on to emulate John Surtees by winning World Championships on both two and four wheels.

Mike's life reads like a novel - and a very racy one. His father Stan was a self-made multi-millionaire who'd earned his considerable riches from building the Kings of Oxford chain of motorcycle dealerships. He had a very forceful personality, could charm the birds off the trees, was a brilliant salesman and publicist, and in his youth dabbled a bit in sidecar racing - the only form of active motor sport that a leg disability would allow. Mike grew up very laid-back, cheerful and music-loving (he played the clarinet and piano well), but he was also rather an introverted chap. Hardly surprising with a man like Stan for a father, although the two of them were always very close.

In the course of messing about in the Kings of Oxford business - after failing to impress academically at Pangbourne Nautical College - it became clear that Mike could ride a motorcycle considerably quicker than most people. This aroused all Stan's suppressed desires for sporting glory. He literally poured money into Mike, aggressively masterminding his racing career, having special bikes made for him, building palatial tuning premises at the family home at Nettlebed, exclusively hiring top engineers, and leaving no stone unturned to force-feed his son's advancement. Unsurprisingly this created jealousy and resentment in the motorcycle racing world, but whilst Mike undoubtedly had enormous advantages he made the most of them. If he hadn't had the talent, all the money in the world wouldn't have made him a winner. Stan's backing just got him there quicker.

A quadruple British champion at the tender age of 18, Mike rapidly became a Honda works rider and, at only 21, was 250cc World Champion. His versatility and skill were awe-inspiring. I've

**Above**: Mike raced Reg Parnell's Lotus BRM V8 at the Nürburgring in 1964.

**Right**: For once without a broad smile on his face, Stanley Michael Bailey Hailwood surveys life from the cockpit of his 1974 Yardley McLaren.

"I'VE SEEN HAILWOOD START FROM THE BACK OF THE GRID WITH AN INJURED LEG AND A PUSHER, AND STILL BEAT A FIELD OF TOP WORLD-CLASS RIDERS."

seen him *at the same meeting* win races on a left-foot gearchange 125cc two-stroke, a right-foot change 250 twin, a 350cc single-cylinder four-stroke and a four-cylinder works MV. I've seen him start from the back of the grid with an injured leg and a pusher to get him going, and still beat a field of top world-class riders. His fluid style was unmistakable and supreme, irrespective of whether it was wet or dry, and he did it all with nonchalant charm and modesty.

And then the floodgates of fame burst open as he became a worldwide sporting icon. He was 500cc World Champion four years in a row from 1962 to '65 for MV, and 250cc and 350cc World Champion for Honda in 1966 and '67. With nine World titles in seven years went dozens of Grand Prix wins and no fewer than 12 Isle of Man TT

victories, at a time when it was by far the most demanding and important motorcycle race in the world. His 1967 500cc Senior TT battle on an evil-handling Honda four against the nimble three-cylinder MV of Italy's Giacomo Agostini (which, ironically, had been developed by Mike) is rightly regarded as one of the greatest races ever, and it had me practically overcome with emotion in the BBC commentary box.

Meantime, looking for fresh fields to conquer, Mike turned his hand to car racing, mixing occasional sports car events and Formula One drives with his motorcycle exploits. But being a superstar on bikes and a part-time tyro in cars was confusing, demotivating and unsuccessful on the car side. So in 1969 he switched to four wheels full-time, with a Formula 5000 and sports car

programme which included driving for the great John Wyer's Ford GT40 team - with no little success, including third at Le Mans.

In 1971 he drove for his former motorcycle rival John Surtees in both F5000 and Formula One. He was runner-up in the F5000 Championship and, in his first F1 Grand Prix for six years, he was one of the four people who crossed the line at Monza within eighteen hundredths of a second in the closest-ever Grand Prix finish. Unfortunately for him he was the last of the group to do so!

By 1972 he was leading almost as busy a life as he had on the bikes. He was European Formula Two Champion, took part in both the Brazilian F2 series and the Tasman F5000 series, and also had his most successful year in Formula One. This included a brilliant drive to second at Monza and a mighty battle for the lead in South Africa with Jackie Stewart's Tyrrell, which only ended when Mike's suspension broke - although he did have the consolation of fastest lap. Things were looking good for 1973, but it was a false dawn. Consistent car unreliability meant not a single point, although Mike distinguished himself by bravely rescuing Clay Regazzoni from his blazing BRM in South Africa. For his gallantry and heroism he was awarded the George Medal.

In a works McLaren Mike drove to four points finishes in 1974 before round 11 at the Nürburgring. And that, sadly, was where his promising Formula One career ended, in a serious accident which badly broke his leg. I went to see him at the hospital after I'd interviewed race winner Regazzoni, who owed his life to Mike, and found him his usual cheerful and phlegmatic self. ("Hello, Muddly, how're you doing?")

Amazingly, though, he wasn't finished with

bikes. He announced his retirement in 1975 and went to live in New Zealand, but he couldn't keep away from the sport he loved so much. In 1978 he made the first of two incredible returns to the Isle of Man. Twenty years after his debut there, he won the Formula One TT on a Ducati. The following year, aged 39, he took an even worthier fourteenth TT victory - the prestigious 500cc Senior race on a Suzuki. I don't think there's ever been a more dramatic motor sporting occasion.

I've said it about Rosemeyer, but I have to say it again. Those they love, the Gods take early. Having finally retired for good, Mike was killed on March 23, 1981 in a road accident for which he was entirely blameless, whilst taking his two children to buy some fish and chips. It was a tragic ending to the life of one of the nicest men I've ever known, and certainly the greatest motorcycle racer there's ever been.

**Above**: The master returns. Eleven years after his last race on the Isle of Man, Mike flew from New Zealand for a "fun" ride in the Formula One TT on a 750cc Ducati. He broke the lap record and cruised to victory, amazed at his continued superiority.

**Far left**: Immaculate style, peerless grace, uncanny speed: in a class of his own in the 1963 Senior race, greatest-of-them-all Mike Hailwood (MV four) rockets to the fifth of his 14 TT wins.

# Jackie
# STEWART

**1965-1973** THE FIRST MODERN F1 DRIVER

Many great drivers, if they've lived long enough to retire, become shadows when they stop racing. It's as though God meant them to be racers, and didn't equip them to do anything else. Their competitive spirit, and their lust for excitement and glamour, cannot find an outlet. They become bored and miserable.

None of that applies to Jackie Stewart. He drove his last race more than a quarter of a century ago, crowning nine years in Formula 1 with 27 victories and three World Championships. All that makes him one of the greatest of all time. Yet since he stopped racing he's been busier than ever. He's played a senior executive role in multi-national companies like Ford and Goodyear. He's become a successful TV commentator and personality, particularly in North America. As a basis for his son Paul's own motor-racing career, he set up a racing team that has achieved unparalleled success in Formula Three, and has put several drivers on the ladder to stardom - including another well-known Scot, David Coulthard. And then in 1995, at the age of 56, he announced that he was going to start his own Formula One team.

To get Stewart Grand Prix off the ground Jackie drew on his long relationship with Ford, and used his prodigious sales skills to attract large sums in sponsorship from blue-chip companies. No-one understood better than he did how tough it is to start up an F1 team, and how many before him had seen their big ideas founder in a sea of debt and disaster. But the very qualities that made Jackie an exceptional racing driver also made him an exceptional manager, and a lot of that rubbed off on his son Paul, who became managing director of Stewart Grand Prix while Jackie filled the role of chairman. His drive to succeed, and his ability to gather round him a strong and talented team, meant that the team not only survived: it became, before the end of its third season, a race winner.

Nowadays Formula One is a matter for huge corporations and billion-dollar budgets, which makes Jackie's achievement all the more astonishing. I believe the history books will show him to be the last individual, as opposed to a major company like Toyota, to have started up an F1 team from scratch. And, fully understanding that life in F1 could only become ever harder for the smaller teams, in 1999 he sold the whole enterprise - for a sum rumoured to be around £80 million - to the Ford Motor Co, who rebadged it as Jaguar.

All this was a long way from the small family garage in Dumbartonshire where the teenage Jackie, a failure at school thanks to undiagnosed dyslexia, served at the pumps. But the will to win was already there: in clay-pigeon shooting he

**Above**: A superb result in Stewart Grand Prix's first season was Rubens Barrichello's second place in the rain at Monaco.

"AS SOON AS JACKIE GOT INTO A SINGLE-SEATER FOR THE FIRST TIME, KEN TYRRELL COULD NOT BELIEVE HOW QUICK, AND HOW SMOOTH, HE WAS."

**Below**: Stewart's sojourn at BRM started brilliantly, but ended with the difficult and unreliable H16. This jump at the Nürburgring in the 1967 German Grand Prix was all for naught: Jackie retired with transmission failure.

found something that he could excel in, and at the age of 16 he was shooting for Scotland. His elder brother Jimmy had been a sports car racer in the 1950s, and soon Jackie persuaded a wealthy customer of the garage to let him race his cars in local events. This led to drives for the national Scottish team Ecurie Ecosse, and his name came to the attention of Ken Tyrrell, who was then planning his Cooper Formula Three team for 1964.

What actually happened was this Scots lad went testing Ecurie Ecosse's elderly Cooper Monaco sports-racer at Goodwood, and the circuit manager, Robin McKay, was so astonished by his speed that he told his friend Ken Tyrrell all about it. Tyrrell phoned Dumbarton and invited the youngster back to Goodwood for a test. As soon as Jackie got into a single-seater for the first

time, Ken could not believe how quick, and how smooth, he was: here clearly was a natural ability which recalled that other Scot, Jim Clark. Ken hired him on the spot, and it was the start of a relationship between the young Scotsman and the tall, no-nonsense timber merchant that, in time, was to take both of them to the top of Formula One.

Jackie swept all before him in F3, winning every race except two (in one of which his clutch failed on the warm-up lap). Not surprisingly, this domination generated offers from no fewer than three F1 teams for the 1965 season. He plumped for BRM alongside Graham Hill, and the results came straight away: a point in his first Grand Prix (Kyalami), a podium in his second (Monte Carlo), second places in his third and fourth (Spa and Clermont Ferrand). At Monza he led his team-

mate over the line to score his first Grand Prix victory, and he finished third in his first World Championship season. It was an astonishing achievement.

The following year Stewart had an accident which was to have a major effect on him, and would indirectly exert a fundamental influence on the future of Formula One. The Belgian Grand Prix on the frighteningly fast old Spa track started in the dry, but it was raining on the far side of the circuit. Seven cars went off as they suddenly ran into the rain on that first lap. Jackie lost control on the notorious Masta Curve, a 150mph kink between two roadside cottages. Hill went off at the same place, scrambled from his BRM unhurt, and ran to the wreckage of his team-mate's car.

Jackie was trapped inside, semi-conscious, and soaked in fuel from a ruptured tank. By the time help arrived and he was removed from the remains of the car, he'd been trapped for almost half an hour. Had there been a fire, it would have been the end of him. In fact he recovered quickly, and was racing again five weeks later: but the crash taught him that many of F1's dangers were avoidable. That was when he vowed to make it his responsibility to improve racing safety.

BRM's great days were past and, though Jackie stayed with them for a third season, his only two finishes were a brave second at Spa, driving with one hand and holding the H16 in gear, and a third in the little V8 BRM on the

Bugatti circuit at Le Mans. However he was still driving for Ken Tyrrell in Formula Two, using a

French Matra chassis, and for 1968 Ken decided to take the plunge and move into Formula One, with a Cosworth DFV-powered Matra. Stewart had an offer from Ferrari, but as soon as he knew Uncle Ken was going into F1 there was no choice: he wanted to be in his team. And now, for wee Jackie, things really began to happen.

He won three Grands Prix that first year with Ken, at Zandvoort, the Nürburgring and Watkins Glen, and finished second in the World Championship. In fact he probably would have won the title, had he not broken his wrist in a Formula Two accident, which forced him to miss two Grands Prix and drive in several more with his wrist in a plastic support. The German victory that year was one of the greatest of his career. The challenging 14-mile circuit was cloaked with

**Above:** Jackie scored six wins out of 11 rounds in the 1971 championship in the Tyrrell 003, and had clinched his second title well before the end of the season.

rain and thick fog, but Jackie, extracting the maximum potential from his new Dunlop rain tyres, led by eight seconds at the end of Lap 1, and 34 seconds at the end of Lap 2. He eventually won the race by over four minutes.

Come 1969 he was virtually unbeatable, winning six out of the first eight races and clinching the title by August. By now Jackie was the complete professional, earning more than anyone in racing had ever done, and always aware of his public image with his fashionable long hair, his dark glasses and his black corduroy cap. And he used his position as the best driver in the world to lead a revolution in racing safety, demanding crash barriers and run-off areas around circuits, better marshalling and medical facilities, and a far greater awareness of the importance of safety from track owners and race promoters. His crusading zeal made him unpopular with many, including some

of his fellow drivers. But those were the days when driver fatalities were horribly frequent, and everyone racing today has reason to be grateful for Jackie's pioneering courage and persistence.

For 1970 Ken Tyrrell decided to build his own car, and until it was ready he used the customer March chassis. It was far from competitive, but Jackie put it on pole position for its first race in South Africa, and managed the marque's first Grand Prix win in Spain. He was now a tax exile in Switzerland, where his friend and neighbour was Jochen Rindt. It was very much Rindt's year: driving the new Lotus 72 the Austrian won four races on the trot. But in practice for the Italian Grand Prix, Jackie's friend was killed when a front brake shaft sheared and sent him into the barriers. Jochen would never know that he was 1970's World Champion.

In 1971, with the Tyrrell now *au point*,

Jackie took six more Grand Prix victories and was Champion again. In 1972 he won four, but a brilliant young Brazilian called Emerson Fittipaldi, who'd replaced Rindt at Lotus, won five and took the title. Then 1973 brought Jackie five wins, eight podiums and his third championship.

By the middle of that year he'd decided to retire. His French team-mate François Cevert, greatly helped by Jackie's guidance, had matured into a fine talent, and was ready to take over as Tyrrell's No 1. In fact three times that season the Tyrrells had finished one-two, and at the Nürburgring, when they finished 1.6 seconds apart, Jackie admitted to Ken later that Cevert could have gone past him if he'd wanted to. Then came further tragedy: in practice for the final round of the year, the United States Grand Prix at Watkins Glen, Cevert crashed and was killed. The Tyrrell team withdrew from the event, and Jackie never raced a car again.

The ensuing three decades have been filled with ceaseless activity for Jackie. I've enjoyed his friendship for all of that time, and I've worked with him many times behind the microphone, notably in Australia, and have marvelled at his eloquence, authority and quick wit. He is equally at home with the young lads of the Springfield Boys Club in the East End of London, where he is the president, as with the royalty of Great Britain and other countries. His energy and application are ceaseless, and above all he is an enormously decent man. And he will tell you that the single win for Stewart Grand Prix - Johnny

Herbert in the 1999 European Grand Prix - means more to him than all of his 27 GP victories as a driver.

At the January 2000 launch of the Jaguar team he announced he was going to retire: but retirement for Jackie means cutting down his workload to that which would fully occupy two or three normal people. He has recently accepted the presidency of the British Racing Drivers' Club, the organisation that owns Silverstone and is responsible for the running of the British Grand Prix. It's a job for which his political skills, business acumen and talent for leadership are ideally suited.

As a driver, Jackie Stewart left Formula One a better place than he found it. He is perhaps the

finest ambassador motor racing has ever had. Now Stirling has his long-awaited title at last, I wonder how long it will be before Jackie gets *his* knighthood? He certainly deserves it.

> "AS A DRIVER, JACKIE STEWART LEFT FORMULA ONE A BETTER PLACE THAN HE FOUND IT."

**Above**: With fourth place at Monza in the Tyrrell 006, Jackie clinched his third world title with two races to go.

# Mario
# ANDRETTI

In the 1952 Italian Grand Prix, while the excited Monza crowd cheered on the Ferraris of Villoresi, Farina, Taruffi and their hero Ascari, a slight, shabby 12-year-old boy pressed up against the fence and marvelled at what he saw. When I become a man, he thought, this was what I will do. But he'd been born into war-time poverty, and had spent much of his childhood in a displaced persons' camp. The wire fence between him and the roaring red cars could not be more impenetrable. How could a poor kid with nothing ever realise his dream to be World Champion?

Yet fairy tales do come true - if they are helped along by iron will, ceaseless determination and unshakeable self-belief. Within 20 years that poor kid would drive, and win, for Ferrari. And within 30 he would be Champion of the World.

Anyone who starts where Mario Andretti started, and achieves what he has achieved, is a hero. Mario is a personification of the American Dream, because his family emigrated to the USA when he was 15, settling in the Pennsylvania town of Nazareth, where he lives still. As soon as they were old enough Mario and his twin brother Aldo started racing stock cars, midgets and sprint cars in local events. Aldo's career was blighted by a serious crash, but Mario went from strength to strength, learning hard lessons in the tough world of American speedway racing. By 1965 the young Italian immigrant was top dog, and over five seasons he was USAC Champion three times and runner-up twice, winning the Indianapolis 500 and, in NASCAR, the Daytona 500.

Back then no USAC driver had ever successfully transferred to Formula One. Few had wanted to try. But Mario's childhood memories of Monza were deep-rooted. He'd met Colin Chapman and Jimmy Clark at Indianapolis, both of whom had been highly impressed with his ability. After Clark was killed in 1968 Colin persuaded Mario into a Lotus 49 for the American Grand Prix at Watkins Glen, and he made history by starting his first Formula One race from pole position.

From then on he did as much Formula One as his USAC commitments would allow, and in 1970 his American sponsors, STP, ran a March for him in five Grands Prix. This was not the competitive car he'd hoped for, and it brought him only one podium, in Spain. But in 1971 he realised the next stage of his dream by signing for Ferrari. His first race for the Scuderia was the South African Grand Prix at Kyalami - and the fairy tale continued, because he won it.

But that was to be his last Grand Prix victory for almost five years, although success continued to come in USAC, sports cars and Formula A. He spent a couple of fruitless F1 seasons with the

**Above**: In the superb ground-effects Lotus 79 Cosworth, Mario Andretti leads his 1978 season-long shadow, team-mate Ronnie Peterson. Andretti took eight pole positions and won six times to become America's second World Champion.

**Above**: Mario's last F1 podium, fittingly, came at Monza, when he put the Ferrari 126C2 on pole position for the 1982 Italian Grand Prix and finished third in the race.

unsuccessful Parnelli team, and then in 1976 he went back to where he'd started in F1, Lotus, and stayed there for five years. Lotus were languishing in seventh place in the constructors' championship when Mario arrived, and during his time there they became champions again. At the end of that period Colin Chapman said that his relationship with Mario - both professionally and personally - was far and away the best he'd had with any driver apart from Jim Clark.

While they worked together, Lotus still had its bad times, with technical culs-de-sac and too many retirements for trivial reasons. But it had its good times, with Mario scoring 11 Grand Prix victories over two years in the black-and-gold cars, and taking the World Championship in 1978. He took little joy from the title, however, because his friend and team-mate Ronnie Peterson was killed on the opening lap of the race that clinched it, the Italian Grand Prix. Mario and Ronnie had spent

much of the season running in convoy at the front of the field, and Lotus were clear winners of the Constructors' Championship. It was the last time they would win it.

By 1981, with another nod towards his Italian roots, Mario joined Alfa Romeo, teamed with Bruno Giacomelli (or Jack O'Malley, as his mechanics used to call him when he started his F1 career with McLaren). But the sum total of a hard year's work for Mario was three points at the start of the year at Long Beach, and then a string of retirements. That was his last full F1 season, and thereafter he concentrated on racing in America, taking another Indycar crown in 1984. By the time he dropped out of the CART circus he had chalked up 407 starts in that class, with 66 poles and 52 victories - an extraordinary record.

There was a Formula One swansong for Ferrari, too. In 1982 he was back at Monza, exactly 30 hectic years after he'd been the kid peering through the fence. To cheers of noisy adulation from the *tifosi* - to whom he has always remained an Italian - he qualified his 126C2 turbo on pole position, and finished a strong third.

Mario's son Mike had an unsuccessful season in Formula One in 1993, but has made a fine racing career in American racing, and is himself a former Indycar champion. But Mario has never quite retired. Always a consummate sports car driver, with many long-distance victories under his belt, he still has one unfulfilled goal: to win the Le Mans 24 Hours. He's done the race many times, and almost won it in 1995, and I have a feeling he hasn't given up on it yet.

His long and incredibly versatile career across so many different racing disciplines has made him the most successful American racer of all time. Through it all Mario has remained a warm-hearted, approachable and courteous man. In all our conversations there has never been any side, or any bull - just his laconic tell-it-like-it-is approach, peppered with a dry, sharp wit. When it's appropriate, he is also capable of surprising eloquence. When he was besieged by the press after Peterson's accident, the only comment they could get out of the newly crowned and grieving champion was one that has been oft-quoted since: "Unhappily, racing is also this."

**Below:** Andretti was a stellar performer in USAC and Indycar racing for an incredible 30 years. This is his Newman-Haas Lola at Elkhart Lake in 1993.

# *Ronnie* PETERSON

## 1970-1978 MR NICE GUY

They always said Ronnie Peterson was far too nice a chap to succeed in Formula One. And, if he'd been around in today's paddocks, that might well have been true. But throughout his brief F1 career his fellow drivers always reckoned he was one of the very fastest. Out of the cockpit he was a shy, gentle individual, but in it he became a ferocious, aggressive force. His towering natural skill and awe-inspiring car control brought in the results almost without Ronnie knowing how, or why.

He was always spectacular to watch, seeming to court disaster with his sideways cornering technique but almost invariably getting away with it. The statistics - 123 starts, 10 wins, 206 championship points - sell him short, for they don't really express his tremendous talent. But Ronnie was no hustler when it came to putting himself in the right place and doing the right deal at the right time. He was just a wonderful driver, and all he needed was the opportunity to show it. Frequently in the wrong car or the wrong team, he didn't get that opportunity often enough.

He was another youngster who forced Formula One to notice him because of his dominating performances in Formula Three and particularly Formula Two - at a time when most of the top F1 drivers did F2 as well, Ronnie frequently beat them. After he won the Monaco F3 race Max Mosley of March signed him up for three years, getting him into F1 in 1970 in a privately-entered March owned by classic car dealer Colin Crabbe.

For 1971 he moved up into the works team. The curious March 711, with its rounded nose and tea-tray front wing, wasn't the most competitive car on the grid beside Ferrari, Tyrrell, Lotus and BRM, but Ronnie's astonishing speed, and his ability to fight his way up the field from lowly grid positions, brought him four second places and a remarkable second place in the World Championship - the best-ever result for a March driver. He was also European Formula Two champion, and a member of Ferrari's sports car team, for whom he won the Buenos Aires and Nürburgring 1000 Kms races.

Escaping finally from his March contract in 1973, he joined Lotus, and became an F1 winner at last. In fact he led 11 of the 15 rounds, and took nine pole positions, but he was less lucky with reliability than team-mate Fittipaldi. Even so he won four Grands Prix that year, and finished third in the championship behind Stewart and Fittipaldi, with Lotus taking the Constructors' Championship.

Then Lotus lost their way with the unsuccessful Type 76, which forced Ronnie to plug on for two more seasons with the old 72 - and win three more Grands Prix with it, including Monaco, and Monza for a second time. By 1976 he was back with March, bringing them their last Grand Prix win - Monza again - before going to Tyrrell to drive

the revolutionary six-wheel P34. This didn't really suit Ronnie's press-on style, and after another indifferent year he returned to Lotus.

Mario Andretti was already installed there as team leader, but Ronnie was perfectly content to drive to orders and run as Mario's No 2, following him home in dominating clean sweeps on four occasions, and winning in South Africa and Austria. They came to Monza clearly first and second in the World Championship. While Mario took pole that weekend, Ronnie had endless problems in qualifying - on the track where he'd won the Grand Prix three times in four years. Then in the Sunday morning warm-up his rear brakes failed. His Lotus 79 flattened three rows of catch fencing and ended up against a tree. Ronnie got out with only bruised legs, but the car was beyond repair, so he had to start the

race in the spare, an old 78.

Starting from the third row, Ronnie was caught by fast starters from behind. As the cars funnelled down from the wide grid area to the narrow entry into the first chicane, a chain reaction led to a multiple pile-up. Several cars spun, and the Lotus was pitched into the guard-rail and caught fire. Hunt, Depailler and Regazzoni got Ronnie out, but the ambulance was slow to arrive. He had serious leg injuries, but apparently nothing life-threatening, and the race was restarted.

It was only next morning that we learned that complications had developed while Ronnie's injuries were being treated in hospital, and he had died. An astounding talent that had promised so much and not yet achieved it had been snuffed out: the nice guy had gone.

**Above:** How we all remember Ronnie: on opposite lock, in a storming full-throttle power slide. This is at Silverstone in the 1971 British Grand Prix, when he conjured a brilliant second place out of the workaday March 711.

# *Niki* LAUDA

## MURRAY'S NOTES

• *Unemotional, intelligent, hard-headed approach combined with impervious self-belief and an ability to make things go his way*

• *Incredible six-week recovery from near-fatal, scarring accident in 1976*

• *Only man to retire, come back - and be World Champion again. Motivated Ferrari into 1970s renaissance, won for Brabham and McLaren too*

## FACTS

**Born**: Vienna, Austria, 22 February 1949
**Grands Prix**: 171
**First Grand Prix**: Zeltweg 1971, March
**Last Grand Prix**: Adelaide 1985, McLaren
**Wins**: 25
**Pole positions**: 24
**Points**: 420.5
**Points per start**: 2.46
**Percentage wins**: 15%
**World Champion**: 1975, Ferrari; 1977, Ferrari; 1984, McLaren

A key ingredient in the make-up of a great racing driver is determination: determination to achieve the goals you set yourself, determination to conquer all set-backs. If there's one man who has had to demonstrate that quality more than anyone else in the history of motor sport, it's Niki Lauda.

Niki was never a conformist. After no great early success in F3 and sports cars, he took out a bank loan to fund a Formula Two season in 1971, and then struggled as a pay driver at the lower end of the F1 grids in 1972 for March, where he was very much in Peterson's shadow, and in 1973 for BRM. But even in the uncompetitive BRM there were flashes of brilliance - like running third at Monaco before the gearbox went - and for 1974 he was invited to join Ferrari alongside the far more experienced Clay Regazzoni.

Ferrari had been without a win for more than a year, but Lauda's determination came to the fore with a relentless schedule of development testing which was beneficial to both car and driver. He was second in his first race for the Scuderia in Argentina, and went on to score wins in Spain and Holland, but there was a string of retirements too. His team-mate Clay Regazzoni was more consistent, and ended up second in the championship, while Niki was only fourth. For 1975 the determined Austrian vowed to do better.

And he did, with a tremendous five-race run from Monaco to France that produced four wins and a second, and assured him of the World Championship - the first for a Ferrari driver since John Surtees more than a decade before. Lauda was set fair to win the 1976 title, too, in a dramatic season-long battle with James Hunt -

with whom he was very friendly off the track: two non-conformists together. He took four wins and two seconds in the first six races, but then, on the old Nürburgring, came the dreadful accident that should have taken his life.

On the second lap his Ferrari suddenly lurched to the right and into the barriers on a fast part of the track, presumably because of some mechanical breakage, and bounced back into the path of Brett Lunger's Surtees. The Surtees hit the Ferrari amidships and pushed it, now on fire, down the track, with the unconscious Lauda still inside. There were no marshals or medical teams nearby, and no safety car in those days, so it was left to other drivers who'd stopped - Guy Edwards, Arturo Merzario, Lunger, Harald Ertl - to wade into the flames and save his life.

Horribly burned, he lay close to death for several days: yet, unbelievably, he turned up at Monza six weeks later, with the burns to his head, face, lungs and upper body far from healed, and insisted on starting the race. His fourth place that day was one of the bravest drives in Formula One's 50-year history.

**Right**: Single-minded, uncompromising and non-conformist, Niki Lauda is truly a very unusual human being.

"LAUDA HAD DECIDED THERE WERE MORE THINGS TO LIFE THAN DRIVING AROUND IN CIRCLES."

Equally brave, and typically Lauda, was his uncompromising decision to withdraw from the final round of the season, the torrentially wet Japanese Grand Prix, after two laps. Fifth place would have been enough to give him the title, but he decided that racing in those conditions was foolish. As a result, he lost the World Championship to James Hunt by one point. The Italian press, who had worshipped him two months before for his comeback, now lambasted him. He showed not the slightest concern: he never cared a fig for what anybody else thought of him, least of all the media. But, having survived a near-fatal accident, he was far more open-minded about the risks than most of his contemporaries. He was able to analyse the danger, weigh it up and look it in the face.

Instead, he silenced his critics by comfortably winning his second World title the following year, winning at Kyalami, Zandvoort and Hockenheim (the German Grand Prix would never again be held on the old Nürburgring, which his accident had shown to be no longer an appropriate track for modern Formula One racing). He then turned his back on Ferrari and went to Bernie Ecclestone's Brabham team for two seasons - and, sensationally, walked out of Formula One before the Canadian Grand Prix because, he said, he'd decided there were more things to life than driving round in circles.

More things in life included starting his own airline, in opposition to the state-owned Austrian Airlines - who tried very hard to make things difficult for him. With the same relentless determination he eventually made it a success, but in those tough early years he realised he still needed the money that F1 had brought. And, to his surprise, he found he was missing the challenge that only Formula One can bring.

So - in a move as surprising as his abrupt retirement - he returned after two years away, accepting a hugely lucrative offer from McLaren.

Right: 1979, Jarama, Spain. After his brilliant 1975-77 spell with Ferrari which gained him two World Championships, Lauda joined Bernie Ecclestone's Brabham-Alfa team in 1978 to partner Nelson Piquet. But it didn't work out. In 1979, with only four points after 13 races, he dramatically left the team in Canada. Three years later he was back as a winner for McLaren.

Other drivers have retired and come back, usually with scant success. When you stop, the F1 world carries on without you, and it's not easy to re-establish your competitiveness. But, to the doubters who said he was past it, Lauda declared he'd be back on winning form within three races. His third race was the Long Beach Grand Prix - and he won it.

He stayed at McLaren for four seasons, won eight more Grands Prix, and - brilliantly - was World Champion for the third time in 1984. Then he went back to his airline, although in the 1990s he found time to be a special adviser to Ferrari. Then in 2001, in a surprising move, he took a senior motor industry job: chief executive officer of Ford's Premier Performance Division, overseeing both the Jaguar F1 team and its engine supplier, Cosworth.

It was an unusual move, but then Niki Lauda is a very unusual man. Added to his extraordinary determination are a razor-sharp brain, a pragmatic approach to life, total self-confidence and an ability to be untouched by the criticisms of others. Behind the clipped, abrupt speech and the apparent lack of emotion, there's also a quirky sense of humour and an extraordinary independence of spirit. He never had any truck with the glamour and prestige of Formula One, and remained unseduced by public glory and the external trappings of success. Every time he won a trophy, he gave it away to his local garage in return for a deal to wash his car once a week.

Even without his recovery from that Nürburgring accident, he would be one of the greats. But that comeback almost from the dead, and the way he nonchalantly wears the visible scars with no thought of cosmetic surgery (which he would regard as a pointless waste of money and effort): all that makes Niki Lauda truly unique.

**Above:** Lauda needed to finish second at the final 1984 round in Portugal to take his third World title by half a point from his young McLaren team-mate Alain Prost. That's exactly what he did.

# James
# HUNT

## MURRAY'S NOTES

• *Towering personality inside which was a sensitive soul with, latterly, doubts about whether he wanted to be racing*

• *Glamorous public figure - brought Formula One to the attention of a new section of the British public*

• *Needed to be happy in his environment to get the best out of his undoubted ability*

## FACTS

**Born**: Belmont, England, 29 August 1947.
**Died**: Wimbledon, England, 15 June 1993.
**Grands Prix**: 92
**First Grand Prix**: Monte Carlo 1973, Hesketh March
**Last Grand Prix**: Monte Carlo 1979, Wolf
**Wins**: 10
**Pole positions**: 14
**Points**: 179
**Points per start**: 1.95
**Percentage wins**: 11%
**World Champion**: 1976, McLaren

There were a lot of James Hunts. James the Racing Driver. James the Commentator. James the Playboy. James the Family Man. James the Hearty, public school and charming. I knew the first two particularly well, but few people knew them all, for he was a very complex person who reached the giddy heights of success, fame and adulation, but also plumbed the depths.

James had a commanding presence and natural dignity. He was larger than life and very outspoken, an immensely likeable human being who didn't think or act like other people. His dress sense was non-existent. For most of his life he drank to excess, he smoked like a chimney, he took drugs. He played as hard as he raced, and he attracted women as much as they attracted him - which was a lot. There was nothing grey about him. Off the track it would be a wild party. On the track it would be all action, but not always racing action. After a collision with David Morgan's March in a televised Formula Three race at Crystal Palace I was astounded to see him run across the track, bristling with rage, and furiously fell his rival. I've seen him do the same to a marshal when the adrenaline was flowing, and his spontaneous outbursts of temper could be terrifying.

He was at the centre of one of the most contentious seasons ever in 1976 when he won his World Championship. After his marriage to the beautiful Susie Miller (who later left him for actor and film star Richard Burton), Mr and Mrs Hunt were splashed across the gossip pages of newspapers around the world, and his good looks, racing success, boisterous personality and enormous charm made him the darling of Britain. His second marriage was as short-lived as his first, but he was a loving and caring father to his two children. He was a brilliant ball-game player (tennis, squash, golf), and generally about as different from today's politically correct and corporate-led Grand Prix drivers as it is possible to be. It is a tragedy that so rich a life ended so soon.

James grew up in a wealthy environment, but after catching the motor-racing bug at a Silverstone club meeting he made his own way in the sport, scratching for money to race a Mini. After a few races he bought a Formula Ford car on hire purchase: that was destroyed in a crash at Oulton Park, but by now others had noticed his speed and he was able to find a sponsored ride, and then move on to Formula Three. Quick he most certainly was - when he was on the black stuff, which he often wasn't. Hence his well-earned nickname "Hunt the Shunt". After the Crystal Palace fisticuffs he was summoned before an RAC Tribunal: but he was found not guilty of incorrect behaviour, while the driver he'd hit lost his racing licence for a year (later reduced under

**Right**: James as we remember him: the long-haired good-time boy who won the World Championship.

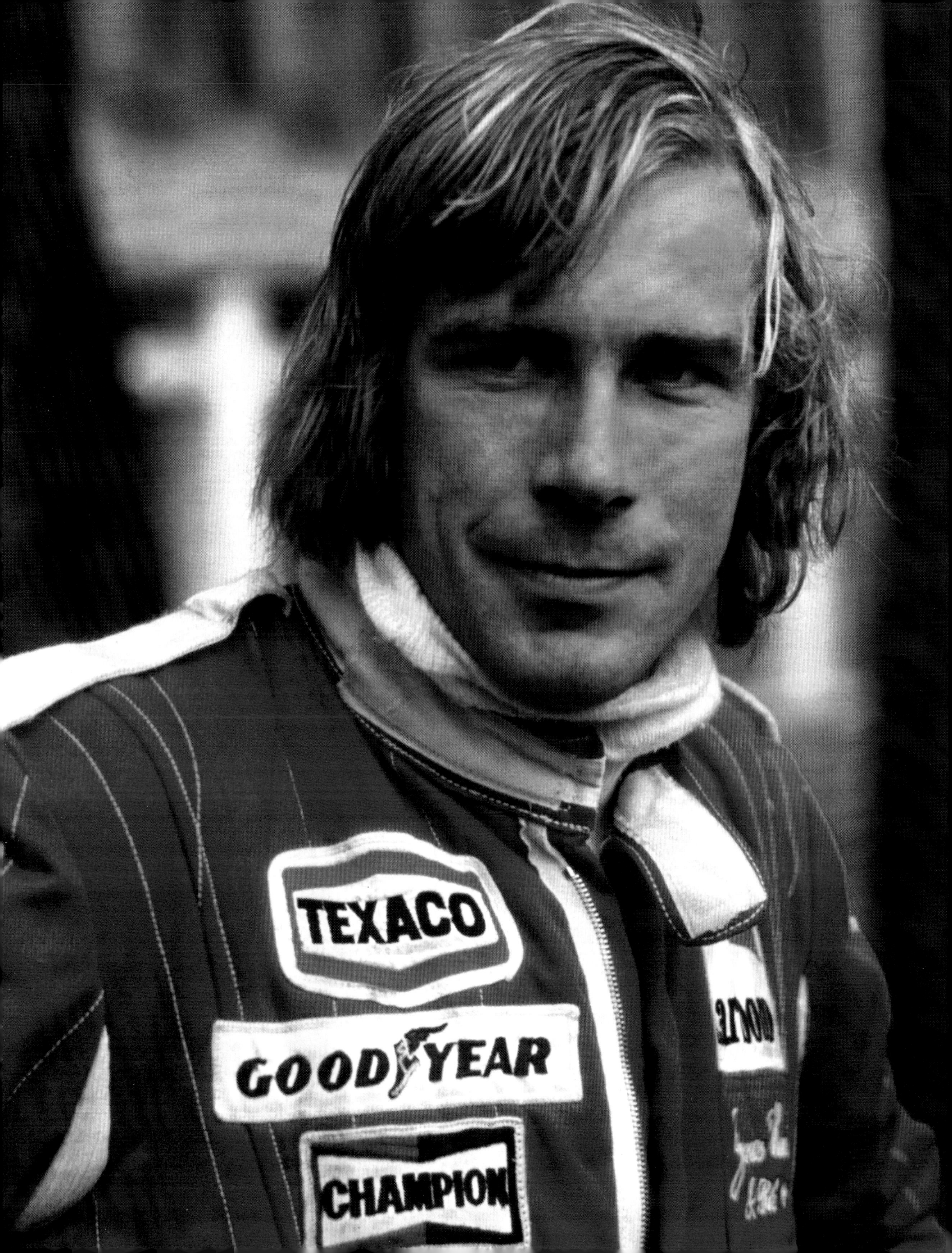
TEXACO
GOOD YEAR
CHAMPION

appeal) for the manoeuvre that had so enraged James. F3 was rough, tough stuff in those days.

But, apart from a reputation for wildness and some major accidents, James had little to show for his first four seasons in motor racing. He was pretty well on his uppers in 1972 when salvation came in the form of Bubbles Horsley, who managed the Formula Three team of the portly, wealthy, eccentric and fun-loving young peer Lord Alexander Hesketh (later, in considerably subdued form, to become Chief Whip in the House of Lords). Bubbles needed a driver as much as James needed a drive, and it was an inspired meeting that was to kick-start a career.

Formula Three led to Formula Two, and then His Lordship decided that Formula One would cost about the same, so that was what they'd do. Which accounted for my delighted reaction when I was invited to partake of smoked salmon and champagne out of the boot of Alexander's Rolls-

Royce at the 1973 Race of Champions at Brands Hatch, where James conducted a Hesketh-hired Surtees to a splendid third place.

Against all expectations, James matured as a driver, and the Hesketh team succeeded. They bought a new March from the factory, and lured away March's chief engineer, Dr Harvey Postlethwaite, to develop it. In seven races the new team achieved a sixth, a fourth, a third, two fastest laps, and then a rousing second on the tail of Ronnie Peterson's Lotus to end the season at Watkins Glen. Beyond all the champagne and the grandiose jokes, there was something special going on here. At the end of the season, for the best performance during the season by a British driver in a British car, James was awarded the Malcolm Campbell Trophy by the RAC - who, three years earlier, had been considering banning him from F3.

For 1974 Postlethwaite designed Hesketh's own very effective Formula One car. With its teddy bear symbol and extrovert ways, this aristocratic *équipe* looked like a glamorous way to spend a lot of money; but underneath the hilarity and high jinks it was deadly serious and extremely competent. With all of Britain enthusiastically behind him, James took his first Formula One win in the 1974 Silverstone International Trophy, and was on the podium at Anderstorp, Zeltweg and Watkins Glen. But it wasn't until the Dutch Grand Prix in 1975 that he scored his first, and Hesketh's only, Grand Prix victory after a stirring battle with Niki Lauda's Ferrari at Zandvoort. There were three more podiums that year, and James finished a rousing fourth in the World Championship.

Then came the bad news. Lord Hesketh decided enough was enough. No more money, and no 1976 drive for James. So it was lucky indeed that McLaren, having lost Emerson Fittipaldi to his brother's Copersucar team, needed someone. James was that someone, and he seized his opportunity. He took pole position for his first race for McLaren in Brazil, and that set the stage for one of the most exciting years in Formula One's history. Against the likes of Lauda, Scheckter, Andretti and Regazzoni he took seven superb wins in Spain, France, Britain, Germany, Holland (in the injured Lauda's absence), Canada and the USA.

It was an incredibly turbulent season. It included disqualification after victory in Spain when the McLaren's rear track was found in post-race scrutineering to be 1.8 cm too wide,

although this win was later re-instated. And it included disqualification after winning in Britain. This was the race at Brands which was stopped after a first-corner pile-up that involved James. At first the officials announced that James would be excluded from the restart; then, after noisy protest from the crowd, he was finally allowed to start - by now his damaged car had been mended - and he duly beat Lauda to win the race. Ferrari protested, and two long months later the FIA upheld the protest. James went on and won the Canadian and American races anyway, so Lauda and Hunt arrived in Japan for the final round with the Austrian three points ahead. The race was torrentially wet: Hunt had tyre problems and could only finish third, but it was enough, for Lauda had withdrawn after two laps. James Hunt had won the World Championship by one point.

Britain went mad with delight, but it was James' zenith. The next year he won at Silverstone, Watkins Glen and Mount Fuji, but McLaren were falling behind in the technology

"JAMES HUNT HAD WON THE WORLD CHAMPIONSHIP BY ONE POINT. BRITAIN WENT MAD WITH DELIGHT."

**Below**: Hunt's first victory in his championship year came in the Spanish Grand Prix at Jarama. In post-race scrutineering the McLaren M23 was disqualified for being too wide, but was reinstated later.

race, and in 1978 he only finished on the podium once, when he was third in France. They were the last championship points he ever scored.

For 1979 he left to join the fledgling Wolf

"LIFE IN THE BOX WITH JAMES WAS NEVER DULL."

team. He did the first seven races of the season, retiring from every one except Kyalami, where he was eighth - and there he had a bad moment when the car's brakes failed completely during qualifying. Formula One had definitely lost its attraction for him, and too many of his colleagues had been injured or died - most recently Ronnie Peterson, whom James had pulled from his burning car at Monza. Immediately after Monaco, depressed and disillusioned, he announced that he had lost motivation and was retiring immediately, after 92 GPs in seven years, 10 victories and a World title. The following year our long BBC partnership began.

It didn't start very well, to tell the truth. I was concerned that I was on my way out, to be replaced by a man I regarded as a drunken Hooray Henry. I was also pretty unimpressed by what I

regarded as a lack of application to his new job. For James, though, it must have seemed a pretty humdrum comedown just to be talking about the drama that until so recently had been his life.

But, inside the commentary box, the chemistry worked. Apparently my enthusiasm and excitement allied to James' knowledge and authority, delivered in that marvellous voice of his, made a good combination, and over the years our initially negative attitudes towards each other changed to one of mutual liking and respect.

Life in the box with James was never dull. At the 1989 Belgian GP he failed to turn up at all, subsequently pleading that he had been in bed with an illness. I was cynical enough to believe that he'd been in bed with something, or rather somebody, else. He was outspoken and provocative about everything, from his hatred of apartheid in South Africa to his low opinion of Riccardo Patrese, Nigel Mansell, and "that French wally" Jean-Pierre Jarier. Of course, the viewers loved it.

I stand up to commentate, but James used to sit down. We shared one microphone, and with both of us thinking we ought to be using it there were some pretty lively scenes in the commentary box - like the time he tugged the cable when I was in full flow, jerked the mike out of my hand, fielded it and laconically started to talk. I was livid, and actually had my fist drawn back to thump him, only desisting when I saw producer Mark Wilkin disapprovingly wagging his finger at me.

James and I worked together for four days at a time, 16 times a year for 13 years. One night before the San Marino Grand Prix, as we were having dinner in a restaurant in Ravenna, the wine waiter arrived, and to my astonishment James ordered orange juice. When I asked why, his cheerful comment was: "I think I've had my share, Murray". I never saw him take another drink. He became very fit, and took up cycling as a way of getting around London. He rode from his home in Wimbledon to the Shepherds Bush studios for our commentary on the Canadian Grand Prix on June 13 1993. He seemed on top of his considerable form: but barely a day later, after a massive heart attack at home, he was dead.

James Hunt packed more into his 45 years than most people could pack into 90, and his death was a tragedy for the countless people to whom his towering personality meant so much. It's a terrible shock when someone young enough to be your son dies totally unexpectedly, and it was with a heavy heart that I gave the address at his memorial service at St James' Church, Piccadilly. I remember him fondly and with regret: because James was truly an unforgettable chap.

**Far left**: Hunt retired with engine trouble at Monaco in 1976, and at this point in the season he was on 15 points, while Niki Lauda had 48 points. His championship chances seemed slender to say the least.

**Below**: James' last half-season was with the Wolf team, and the boxy WR7 brought him no joy. At Long Beach he failed to complete a racing lap.

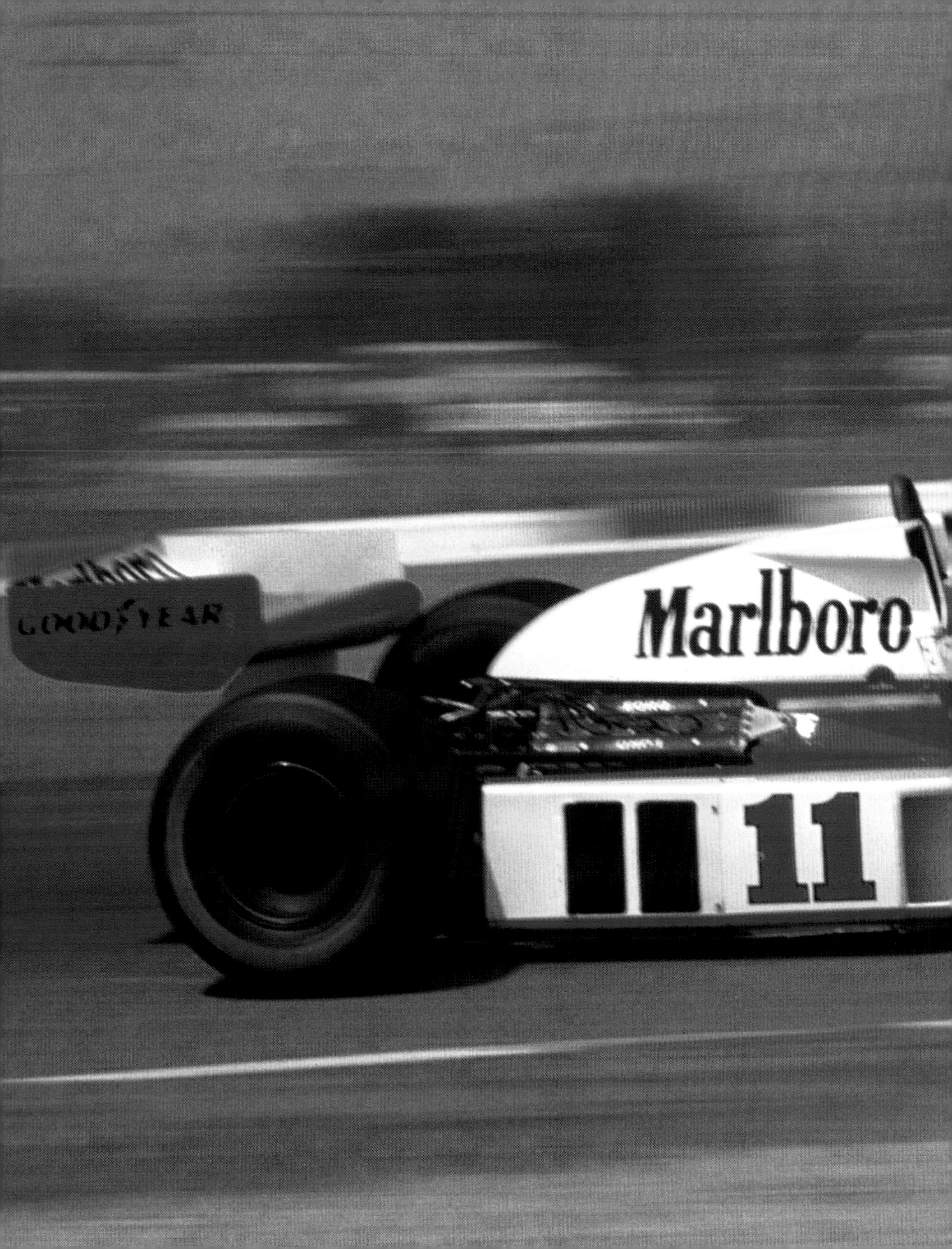
GOODYEAR
Marlboro
11

# Alan
# JONES

Sporting heroes often display their national characteristics to extremes. Think of most people's concept of the Australian male, and you come up with words like tough, uncompromising, humorous, plain-speaking, determined and sheer bloody-minded. With each of those adjectives, you could be describing Alan Jones.

Some like Alan, some loathe him. I'm very much in the former category, and for me it's those same rough tough qualities that make him one of the modern heroes of F1. I knew him well throughout his racing career, and have worked with him many times since, in the commentary box at the Australian Grand Prix. He's very refreshing - direct, tells it like it is, and certainly doesn't mince his words. Which is just how he always was as a World Champion. In the F1 paddocks, the more feathers he ruffled, the happier he was.

Alan comes from a motor-racing family. His father Stan Jones was a tough guy too. He raced a Maserati 250F and the ferocious locally-brewed Maybach Special, and won the Australian and New Zealand Grands Prix. On his day he beat Jack Brabham, and he died still regretting that he'd never tried his luck on the world stage by pulling up his roots and coming to Europe. He was a car dealer, and while Alan was growing up he was doing very well. Alan by his own admission was a spoilt kid who got pretty much whatever he wanted, including karts to race - he was a class champion at 15 - and an MG for his 16th birthday. As soon as he was old enough he was racing his dad's Cooper-Climax, and winning in that too.

Then Stan's business went bust, and suddenly Alan found out about the harder side of life. But he followed his dream and came to England, with £50 in his pocket. He found a room in a basement flat in Earl's Court and started dealing in cars by the roadside, selling old vans to Australian tourists, living hand to mouth and saving every penny. In a year he'd got enough cash to buy an old Formula Ford and go racing, but that was written off in a test session by a friend. More vans got sold, and Alan managed to buy an old F3 Lotus. This was written off in a test session, too, breaking Alan's leg. But Alan was made of determined stuff. He found another car and stuck it out in Formula Three, eventually getting enough backing to run in Formula Atlantic and then Formula 5000. He had his good races, he had his bad races, but all the while the hand-to-mouth existence of the impoverished British racer was blending with his inbred Aussie toughness to build a case-hardened character.

His break into F1 came in 1975 in a privately-entered Hesketh run by former F3 driver Harry Stiller. In four races he had two accidents and a wheel fall off, and then in the fourth he finished

Right: A familiar 1980 sight! Alan triumphantly raises his winner's trophy after the USA East GP at Watkins Glen.

"JONES DEVELOPED A WONDERFUL RAPPORT WITH FRANK WILLIAMS AND PATRICK HEAD, AND THEY BECAME ALMOST INDOMITABLE."

11th a lap behind. Stiller pulled out, but Rolf Stommelen had been injured while driving for Graham Hill's Embassy team, so Alan filled in there for four races - and scored two points with a doughty fifth place at the Nürburgring, the best finish the Hill marque ever had. This could have led to a full-time seat, but that November Graham Hill and his No 1 driver Tony Brise perished in a plane crash.

So Alan moved to Surtees, picking up a fourth and two fifths, but the relationship between those two strong characters, AJ and Big John, was always going to be stormy. Alan's fourth place in Japan at the end of the season was his last drive for the team, and he left Surtees without regret. The 1977 season started with Jones kicking

slow. But Alan provided the upset of the season when he beat Niki Lauda's Ferrari to win the Austrian Grand Prix - the only win Shadow ever had. People were now waking up to what Jones was capable of, even in lesser equipment, and as a result Ferrari produced a contract for Alan for 1978...and, at the last moment opted for Gilles Villeneuve instead.

Thus Alan ended up with Williams, another team which at the time was midfield at best. Their highest placing in the Constructors' Championship was ninth, and they'd never won a Grand Prix, or even come near to doing so. But, like Clark and Lotus or Stewart and Tyrrell, this was the start of one of the great driver/team relationships in F1. During Alan's four years there, Williams grew up as a team, and Alan grew up as a driver. He developed a wonderful rapport with team boss Frank Williams and designer Patrick Head, and they became almost indomitable.

That first year Williams was a one-car team, and the best result was Alan's second place to Reutemann's Ferrari at Watkins Glen. For 1979 it was a full two-car team and Patrick Head's brilliant FW07 looked like a winner from the start. After leading at Zolder and Silverstone (where his team-

Above: Jones scored his first championship points by finishing fifth at the Nürburgring in 1975, driving for Graham Hill's Embassy team.

his heels, but then Welshman Tom Pryce died at Kyalami, and Shadow drafted in Alan as his replacement. It wasn't a great seat: the team was short of funds and the car was overweight and

mate Clay Regazzoni scored Williams' first win after he'd retired), Jones won Hockenheim, Zeltweg and Zandvoort on the trot, and finished third in the World Championship. But 1980 was

when it all came together for the Didcot team. After five tremendous victories Alan was crowned World Champion, with Williams Constructors' Champions. The combination of a brilliant ground-effects car, a superbly managed team and a hard charger in the cockpit had taken Williams in two seasons from shoestring also-rans to the top of the heap.

Tired of the relentless Formula One schedules and missing his native land, Jones decided to retire from Grand Prix racing at the end of 1981. He scored a storybook victory in Las Vegas in what was to have been his last race. Back home in Australia he did some national racing, but like others before and since he found he missed the adrenaline rush of F1, and made two unhappy efforts to return. In 1983 he agreed to join Arrows, but left after one race; and in 1985 he

signed to drive for the new, and rich, Beatrice team from the USA, run by veteran entrant Carl Haas. It was an expensive disaster: as others have discovered coming fresh to the cruel world of Formula One, money alone is no guarantee of even the slenderest results. Alan did 19 races and managed one fourth and one sixth before calling it a day.

Today he remains close to the sport back in Australia, both through touring car racing and overseeing the racing career of the third Jones generation, his son Christian. Meanwhile, at Williams Grand Prix the current tally of Drivers' and Constructors' world titles now numbers 16. But, 20 years on, Frank and Patrick still talk fondly of their first championship year, and of the tough Aussie who called a spade a bloody shovel, and always drove his heart out, whatever the odds.

**Above**: Championship year. Jones on his way to victory in Montreal in the 1980 Canadian Grand Prix, one of five wins that helped give Alan the title and Williams their first constructors' title.

# Gilles VILLENEUVE

**1977-1982** FOR THE LOVE OF RACING

Had Gilles Villeneuve been born in an earlier racing generation, when sheer courage and racing attack played a bigger role in success than they do today, he could have been World Champion. As it was, in terms of results he achieved less in his whole racing career than his son Jacques achieved in his first two F1 seasons. Apart from his single debut race for McLaren, Gilles spent his entire Formula 1 career with Ferrari. He won six Grands Prix for them, but in the championship he never again approached the result of his second year, when he was runner-up to team-mate Jody Scheckter. However, if you were to grade all my heroes by the nebulous and over-worked measure of charisma, Gilles would be near the top of the list.

He was another who refused to fit into the accepted mould of the Formula One driver. Eschewing expensive hotels and private planes, he preferred to go from race to race in a motorhome, in which he would live during race weekends with his wife Joann and two young children, Melanie and Jacques. More perhaps than anyone in the history of Formula One, he raced simply because he loved it: he just happened to love driving cars on the limit, and sometimes over the limit. And he was very good at it. He was an uncomplicated racer and, at a time when F1 was already becoming more professionalised and businesslike, he was like a visitor from a bygone age.

He came up through snowmobile racing in his native Canada - which left him with a prodigious talent on a slippery track - and then Formula Ford and Formula Atlantic. Other teams might have found his wild style hard to take, which helps explain why, after a single trial race for McLaren

in 1977, he stayed with Maranello till the end. Enzo Ferrari, that difficult and devious old man, loved Gilles like a son, and warmed to his uncomplicated approach.

He had a lot of accidents, some of which were his fault, some of which weren't. In his second race for Ferrari he collided with Peterson's Tyrrell and somersaulted into the crowd, killing two spectators. But he matured quickly, although that first season was punctuated with spins, accidents and retirements. Then, in the final round of the year, came his historic first victory in his home Canadian Grand Prix. His win was greeted by the Canadian people with scenes of national ecstasy: in my first full year of Formula One TV commentating, I'd never seen anything like it. The scenic Montreal track is called Le Circuit Gilles Villeneuve to this day.

In 1979 the Ferrari 312T4 was the class of the field, and for the last time for more than 20 years a Ferrari driver won the World Championship. On six occasions Gilles led team-mate Jody Scheckter home, winning at Kyalami, Long Beach and Watkins Glen, but the South African finished more races and took the title. One incident which planted Gilles in the memory of every F1 fan was at Zandvoort that year, when he came through brilliantly from sixth

on the grid to lead by lap 11, and pulled away - until one of his rear tyres developed a slow puncture.

Losing pace, he clung on to the lead, pushing his bucking, sliding Ferrari as hard as it would go, until the inevitable happened and it spun out of control in a cloud of rubber smoke. Gilles got it pointing the right way and resumed, but instead of coming into the pits for fresh tyres he raced on, now second and chasing leader Alan Jones. A lap later the tortured tyre finally exploded. Gilles spun the car to a halt, and then after a three-point turn got back on the track and drove on in a shower of sparks - at no mean speed. Somehow he made it to the pits, where Ferrari boss Mauro Forghieri threw up his hands in horror at the damage and motioned Gilles out of the car. The little Canadian just hated to give up.

In contrast to its predecessor, the 1980 Ferrari T5 was a dog, but Gilles tried as hard as ever, with little result. In 1981, with Ferrari using turbo power for the first time, he scored back-to-back victories in Monte Carlo and Spain - strangely the only Grands Prix he ever won in Europe. At Imola in 1982, during a dispute between the FIA and the F1 constructors, most of the British teams boycotted the San Marino Grand Prix, and it was clearly going to be a Ferrari walkover. Villeneuve and his team-mate Didier Pironi decided they would put on a show for the crowd and finish in that order, but right at the end Pironi failed to keep to their agreement, blocking Villeneuve's attempts to get his lead back. Gilles was furious, and never spoke to him again. Thirteen days later, towards the end of qualifying for the Belgian Grand Prix, Gilles found himself slower than the hated Pironi. He went out to beat his time, and rocketed over a brow to find Jochen Mass's slowing March. The two cars touched and Villeneuve's Ferrari cartwheeled over the fences, throwing him out and killing him instantly. He was perhaps the last old-fashioned racer in F1. His death marked the end of an era.

**Above**: The famous Zandvoort incident in 1979, when Gilles wanted to keep on racing even as his Ferrari fell to pieces around him.

**Far left**: Gilles Villeneuve raced purely for the love of the sport, and it was always enthralling to watch him at work.

# Keke ROSBERG

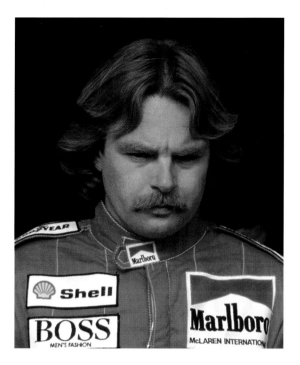

Alan Jones' abrupt retirement from Formula One at the end of the 1981 season left a gap in the Williams team, and it was a surprise when Frank chose a moustachioed Finn called Keijo "Keke" Rosberg as his replacement, alongside Carlos Reutemann.

Keke, three times Finland's kart champion, had raced in various single-seater formulae in Europe, North America and New Zealand. He already had four F1 seasons under his belt, but for lesser teams such as Theodore, ATS, Wolf and Fittipaldi, and with little in the way of results, although there had been definite flashes of talent - like winning the rain-drenched Silverstone International Trophy in 1978, almost his first F1 race; and getting on the podium in Argentina in 1980.

In fact Keke was just waiting for the right equipment to show what he was capable of. In his first race for Williams he was fifth, and in his second he was second, although later disqualified for being underweight. Then, two races into the season, the mysterious Mr Reutemann unaccountably decided to walk away from F1, and Keke found himself pitchforked from habitual non-qualifier for Fittipaldi a few months before to team leader at Williams.

He rose heroically to the occasion. He was second at Long Beach, Zolder and Zeltweg, and third at Zandvoort and Hockenheim. Then he scored a very canny victory in the Swiss Grand Prix (held in France at Dijon, because circuit racing has been illegal in Switzerland ever since 1955). This was an unusual season, and a sad one: Ferrari were stricken by tragedy when first Gilles Villeneuve was killed at Zolder and then, three months later, Didier Pironi

was so badly injured at Hockenheim that he never raced again. McLaren, with Lauda and Watson, and Renault, with Prost and Arnoux, spread most of the spoils amongst themselves, but they suffered reliability problems too - and all the while the ever-consistent Rosberg was clocking up the points, scoring in 10 races. Despite having only one win - against two each for Watson, Pironi, Prost and Lauda - he took the World title by five points.

In 1983 the turbo era had really arrived, and the normally-aspirated Williams was not so competitive, but Keke scored a brilliant win at Monaco, running on slicks throughout a damp race and displaying all his awesome Scandinavian car control. By 1984 Williams was Honda turbo-powered, and Rosberg was in his element. As much as anyone he wrung the maximum out of these difficult, harsh cars, and was always tremendously spectacular to watch. I for one will never forget the sight of Keke qualifying for the British Grand Prix in 1985, the last one for which the old flat-out Woodcote was unsullied by a chicane. Spots of rain were starting to fall as Keke took the Williams by the scruff of the neck and threw it through the corner, teetering on the edge of control at almost 170 mph. His average speed

for the whole lap was 160.9 mph, and it gave him the fastest ever pole position in a British motor race ahead of Senna, Prost, Piquet, Mansell and all the rest.

Three more Williams wins came his way, including a particularly impressive drive in the crushing heat of Dallas in 1984, and nicely-paced victories in Detroit and Adelaide in 1985, when he was third in the World Championship behind Prost and Alboreto and ahead of Senna.

In 1986 he went for his last season to McLaren alongside Alain Prost. He was determined to win the final race of his career in Australia, and he sought me out before the start. Now, my reputation for saying things are going well for a driver just before it all turns bad is as well known in the F1 paddock as it is in the nation's living rooms. "Murray," said Keke, "You know this is my last race. If I am doing well, for God's sake don't say

anything. I don't want to suffer from the Curse of Murray Walker." Well, he came through from seventh on the grid to put himself in a solid lead, and of course I had to tell the viewers that Rosberg was leading his last race. With 20 laps to go a tyre burst, and it was all over...

Having retired as a driver, Keke flung himself into the business side of motor sport, in particular as a team boss in touring cars and as a highly successful drivers' manager, most notably of double World Champion Mika Hakkinen. His amiable personality fronts well-developed negotiating talents, sharp business acumen and a shrewd analytical brain. Ask Keke for his views on any current Formula One issue or conflict, and you will get a witty, realistic and highly intelligent review of the factors involved - rounded off with a dose of good-humoured cynicism. In today's self-important F1 paddock, Keke Rosberg is an appreciating asset.

**Above**: Rosberg coped brilliantly with slicks on a damp track to win the 1983 Monaco Grand Prix. In this Saturday practice shot, when it was raining, he is on wet-weather rubber.

**Far left**: Rosberg spent his last season as a McLaren driver, and so nearly won his final race in Adelaide.

"'IF I AM DOING WELL, FOR GOD'S SAKE DON'T SAY ANYTHING. I DON'T WANT TO SUFFER FROM THE CURSE OF MURRAY WALKER.'"

# Nigel MANSELL

Silverstone, 1977. "Come with me", said ace talent-spotter John Thornburn. "I want you to meet someone who's going to the top." I went, because John knows what he's about. The man I was introduced to was a 24-year-old, in his second season of Formula Ford, called Nigel Mansell. "Pleasant chap", I thought. "He's a Brummie from Hall Green, like me." I was to see a lot more of him over the next 18 years.

Nigel had come from an impressive apprenticeship in karts and, despite breaking his neck, he did well in Formula Ford - well enough to fight his way into Formula Three. It has become legend that he quit his job, sold his house to pay for a March F3 drive, relied on his loyal and charming wife Rosanne to be the breadwinner, and caught the eye of no less a person than Colin Chapman. It was after damaging his spine that the call came to test for the Lotus Formula One team. Nigel stuffed himself full of pain killers, and got the drive.

The years of sacrifice and denial were to prove a great investment. Nigel went on to become statistically Britain's most successful racing driver, with 31 victories and 482 points out of 187 Grand Prix starts. He was World Champion in 1992, spent two seasons with Ferrari - every racing driver's dream - and added to all that the unique achievement of winning America's demanding Indy Championship in his first year.

Nigel is an extraordinary mixture. In the cockpit he was inspired: gutsy, single-mindedly determined, awesomely brave and with an implacable will to win. He gave me more magic commentary moments than all the rest of them put together, because wherever he was there was drama and excitement. Collapsing in the searing heat of Dallas as he tried to push his broken Lotus to the finish. Passing Senna's McLaren in his Ferrari to win in Hungary. Unbelievably taking Gerhard Berger on the outside of Mexico's notorious Peraltada. Losing a wheel in the pitlane in Portugal. Jinking past Nelson Piquet at Stowe to win the 1987 British Grand Prix. Grimly parallelling Senna in Spain, wheel-to-wheel with sparks flying at 200 mph, until Ayrton backed off. Losing the 1986 World Championship in Adelaide when a tyre blew at 190 mph. Taking a sensational second place at a sodden 1988 Silverstone in a car that truly wasn't capable of it. The last laps of Monaco in 1992 when he all but drove over the top of Senna's McLaren in his fruitless bid to win. His dramatic departure from Williams. The physical confrontation with Senna in Belgium. Black-flagged in Portugal for reversing in the pitlane. The list just goes on and excitingly on.

Not only that: Nigel was a brilliant showman. He has always seen himself as a man of the

**Right:** "He loves them and they love him," I shouted into the microphone ecstatically and it was true. Nigel warmed to the adulation he received for his gutsy driving and returned it on the podium, in the pitlane and wherever he met his adoring public.

"NIGEL MANSELL
IS A REAL FRIEND
WHOSE WARM
FAMILY HOSPITALITY
IT HAS BEEN MY
VERY GREAT PLEASURE
TO EXPERIENCE
MANY TIMES."

people, and he loves them. He plays to the crowd, never fails to give an autograph, happily chats with his multitude of fans, and exploits every opportunity to bond with them.

All perfect, then? Well, no, actually. Are any of us? Nigel is amazingly thin-skinned and easily offended. The in-crowd of Formula One saw him as a chip-on-both-shoulders whinger with a persecution complex who was forever complaining about anything and everything. It certainly isn't hard to fall out with him, and lots of people have done so. But, on a speak-as-you-find basis, I certainly have no complaints, for he was and is a real friend whose warm family hospitality it has been my very great pleasure to experience many times.

That Lotus test drive in 1980 was a turning point in Mansell's career, for Colin Chapman became his friend and mentor. He saw in Nigel both an incredibly focused man with total self-belief, and a gifted driver with enormous potential, and he was so right. He made his protégé a millionaire but, although Nigel drove for Lotus for five years, the team was in the doldrums at that time, between the glories of Andretti and Senna. So, although there were outstanding podiums, like his 1981 Zolder fight with Gilles Villeneuve, and near misses like Monaco 1984 ("I crossed a white line, Murray, and it just slid away from me"), his best results from 59 Grands Prix were five third places. When Chapman died in 1982 Nigel's days at

Lotus were numbered. Peter Warr was in charge now, and they didn't get on. So goodbye Lotus, hello Williams.

And that was where Nigel finally came good, with a vengeance. In two spells totalling six seasons with Frank and Patrick's team, he would score 28 Grand Prix victories for them. In 1985 he ran alongside Rosberg, and after a slow start he ended that first Williams season with resounding victories at Brands Hatch in the European Grand Prix - Nigel's first real taste of the power of his adoring British supporters - and a fortnight later in Kyalami. For 1986 Piquet replaced Rosberg, ostensibly as No 1, and won four races, but Mansell won five. As the teams went to the final round in Adelaide he had a six-point lead over McLaren's Alain Prost, and the World title was

within his grasp. With 19 laps to go his rear tyre exploded, and his dream was shattered.

It was so near yet so far in 1987, too. This time Nigel scored six victories, to Piquet's three, but Piquet's seven second places put him ahead on points. Then in practice for the penultimate round in Japan Nigel crashed, injuring his back, and was out for the rest of the season. Second in the championship again.

Williams 1988 was no place to be if you were a winner. They had been abandoned by Honda and were struggling with off-the-pace Judd V8 power. And, at that point, Nigel still hadn't won the world title he fervently believed he deserved. So, after a lacklustre season and an irresistible offer from Ferrari, he went to Italy. The fanatical *tifosi* took him to their hearts - especially when,

**Above**: One of the great Mansell moves was when he sold a dummy to Williams team-mate and rival Nelson Piquet three laps from the end of the 1987 British Grand Prix to score a victory that sent the crowd mad with joy. Here he lines up the Brazilian in his sights.

**Far left**: At Adelaide in 1986, Mansell leads Senna's Lotus, Piquet's Williams and the McLarens of Prost and Rosberg. His championship chances disintegrated along with his left rear tyre on lap 63.

against all the odds, he won his first race for the Prancing Horse in Brazil. They called him *Il Leone*, the Lion, and when he breathtakingly swooped

**Above**: Ambition finally achieved. On the Hungarian podium after finishing second, Nigel comes to terms with the fact that he is 1992 World Champion. Long-time rival Senna (right) offers congratulations.

past his eternal rival Ayrton Senna to win in Hungary their joy knew no bounds.

Nigel was the last driver to be personally appointed by Enzo Ferrari, and at first he fitted in well at Maranello. But it all came unglued in 1990 when Alain Prost replaced Gerhard Berger as his team-mate. Nigel believed, amid what he saw as Machiavellian intrigue, that the team was favouring the Frenchman. By mid-season Prost had scored four victories, the fourth when Mansell's gearbox cost him victory in the British Grand Prix by developing a mind of its own. It was the last straw. There and then, throwing his gloves into the Silverstone crowd in a typically theatrical gesture, Nigel announced he was retiring from the sport.

Until: enter Frank Williams, with a fulsome promise to satisfy every one of Nigel's considerable demands. Now in their third year with the impressive Renault V10 engine, Williams

were winners again. Actually, it took Nigel a bit of time to get back into his stride with Frank's team. For the first half of the season he was consistently out-qualified by team-mate Riccardo Patrese, who beat him in a Williams 1-2 in Mexico. But then it all came together: first in France, first for an emotional third time in Britain, first in Germany and Italy. There was the drama in Portugal when an untightened wheel came off in the pitlane after a tyre stop, then another win a week later in Barcelona. At the end of it all Mansell was second in the championship to Senna, and the stage was set for that wonderful all-conquering Championship year of 1992.

He began it by winning the first five races of the year on the trot, a feat unbeaten since the days of Alberto Ascari 40 years before. By the end of the year he'd made it nine victories, an all-time record of wins in one year since equalled by Michael Schumacher, but still unbeaten. There was another emotionally-charged victory at Silverstone - this time Nigel led from pole position to chequered flag - and by August, with five races still to go, he'd clinched the championship and achieved his life's ambition.

But the year ended in tears. Nigel was devastated to learn that the hated Alain Prost was to join Williams for the following year, and then he found himself unable to agree his remuneration deal with the team for 1993. At Monza on race morning Nigel called a press conference, and made the dramatic announcement that he was quitting Formula One. Disgusted with what he saw as unreasonable treatment by the team for whom he'd won 28 races and a World Championship, he'd decided to try a different challenge, and was America-bound for the CART series.

Fresh fields to conquer, then, and conquer them he certainly did. With a string of superlative victories for the Newman-Haas team, especially on the fearsome ovals which he had never even seen before, Nigel shattered the American establishment by winning the championship in his Rookie year, and very nearly winning the fabled Indianapolis 500 at his first attempt.

Then, to general amazement, he signed for McLaren in 1995. But, disappointed with the car's performance, he drove in only two races before contentiously fading away.

Fifteen years in Formula One is a very long time. Driving for Lotus, Williams and Ferrari, Nigel Mansell made an impact on it like few before him, and brought a huge number of new British fans into the sport. He achieved an astonishing amount in the USA, too, despite his short time there. He has never formally retired - there has even been the occasional foray into touring car racing - but now, as a very wealthy man and a fanatical golfer, he works as tirelessly

**Below**: Red Five had a brilliant debut season in Indycar racing in 1993. Mansell won the opening round in Surfers Paradise, scored four further wins, came near to winning the Indianapolis 500, and beat Emerson Fittipaldi to the Indycar Champion's title.

Amazing. His second Stateside season was a comparative failure but, in a four-race return to Formula One for Williams following Ayrton Senna's death, he showed he had lost none of his powers by winning the final round in Australia.

as he did in Formula One to develop his superb golf and health club complex at Woodbury Park, near Exeter. After a colourful career that few can match, he is gone from motor sport, but he is certainly not forgotten.

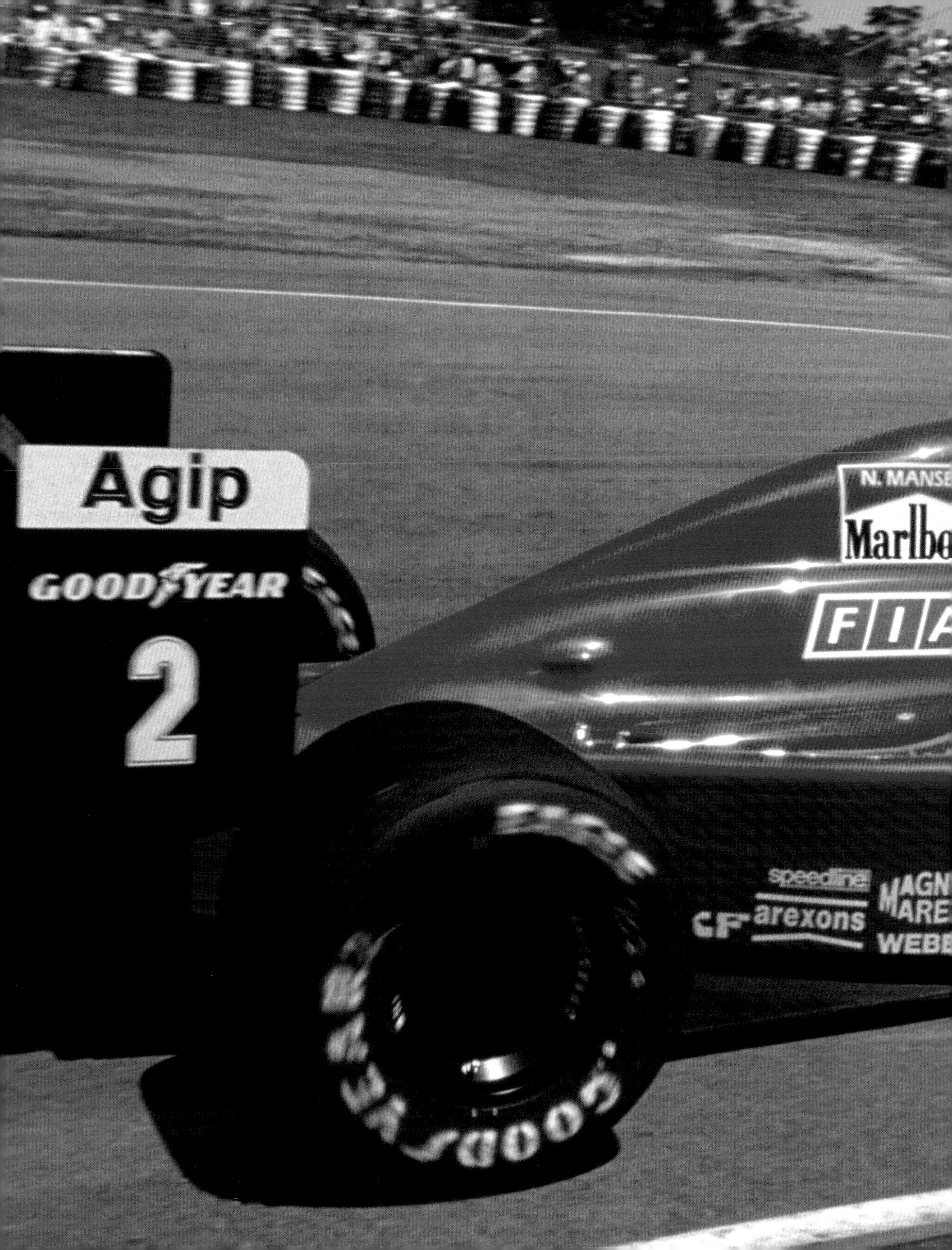

Agip
GOODYEAR
2
N. MANSE
Marlb
speedline
arexons
WEBE

# Alain PROST

If greatness were just a matter of statistics, Alain Prost would stand head and shoulders above the rest. He raced in Formula One for 13 seasons, and won 51 Grands Prix - more than a quarter of the 199 he started, and a total no other driver has approached. He was World Champion four times, more than anyone else except Fangio, and racked up an unbeaten total of 798.5 points. That's an average of four points every race - like finishing on the podium every single time! - and during that golden period he had to race against the likes of Lauda, Piquet, Mansell, Senna and Schumacher to do it.

But there's more to being a Formula One Hero than mere statistics. Alain Prost was a perfectionist, a man who approached every part of the job of going motor racing with care and deep thought. Not for nothing was his nickname The Professor. He was always hugely quick, but he was never the most spectacular driver to watch. Smooth, disciplined and controlled, he tended not to be the driver whose exploits you talked about at the airport, waiting for the plane home after the race. But he'd usually beaten all the men you *were* talking about!

Prost had in spades the burning will to win and unshakeable motivation that drive all great champions. But in his case it was combined from the start with a quietly-spoken common sense, a strong awareness of what he believed was right and wrong, and a refusal to take risks for no purpose. For example, he was honest about his dislike of racing in the rain: he could be very quick on a wet track if he had to be, but he was prepared to stick by his principles and withdraw if he

thought conditions were needlessly dangerous - as he did in Australia in 1989.

Alain also possessed remarkable political and diplomatic skills, and was a past-master at gathering the entire personnel of a team around him - as Nigel Mansell found to his dismay when Prost joined him at Ferrari in 1990. He even out-manoeuvred the politically astute Ayrton Senna when both were vying for Mansell's seat at Williams in 1993. He was always adroit in his handling of the media, too. I must have interviewed him hundreds of times, and always he was patient, direct, courteous and good-humoured - all part of his professionalism and attention to detail.

Prost's early career followed the classic route: teenage success in karting leading to victory in the European Championship, then French and European titles in Formula Renault and Formula Three. He was already 25 when, in 1980, he made his F1 debut for McLaren, finishing in the points in his first two races. Then he moved to Renault for three seasons. The yellow cars weren't very reliable, but they were fast, and when Alain finished it was

**Right**: Prost's 28th Grand Prix victory put him ahead of Stewart in total wins, but he went on to hit a record-setting total of 51.

PROST

P 1

28

"ALAIN PROST

WAS A PERFECTIONIST,

A MAN WHO

APPROACHED EVERY

PART OF THE JOB

WITH CARE AND

DEEP THOUGHT."

usually on the podium. Appropriately, his first Grand Prix victory came in this French car in the French Grand Prix at Dijon in 1981, and he won at Paul Ricard again in 1983. There were seven other Renault victories, and in 1983 Prost was runner-up for the title, just two points behind Piquet.

Then he returned to McLaren to join Niki Lauda, and the old fox and the young charger shared the glory between them. Prost was brilliant that year, winning seven races, but he only got half points for his Monaco victory because the race was shortened by rain. In the end he had to cede the title to Lauda by just half a point. But in 1985 he was conclusively champion, by a margin of

run thing, for Mansell was only beaten when his tyre blew in the final round. Williams-Honda were dominant in 1987, but Prost scored three more victories; and then in 1988 he found himself with a new team-mate, Ayrton Senna.

This looked like the perfect super-team, particularly as McLaren now had Honda power as well. But, as others have found, putting the two best drivers in the same outfit can be a recipe for disaster. As far as McLaren was concerned it was a total success, with the red and white cars winning a record 15 out of 16 races, and at first relations between Alain and Ayrton were cordial. That first year, while Prost was the more consistent, Senna won more races, and took the title by two points.

But by 1989 the two drivers were at outright war, culminating in the McLarens crashing into each other in the penultimate race in Japan. Prost retired on the spot, while Senna restarted and won the race. Then he was disqualified, so the title was Prost's.

But Alain had had enough of the tense atmosphere within the team. After six consecutive years with McLaren, he left for Ferrari. His first

**Above:** The patriotic first F1 victory for Prost was in the all-French Renault turbo RE30 in the French Grand Prix at Dijon in 1981.

20 points from Ferrari's Michele Alboreto. He repeated the feat in 1986, to become the first back-to-back champion since Jack Brabham over 25 years before, although this time it was a closer

year at Maranello seemed to revitalise the team, and he was on brilliant form. He won five Grands Prix, finished second in two and third in two. The championship was once more between himself

and Senna. But, incredibly, it was all resolved once more by a collision with Senna in Japan, and this time Senna took the title as a result.

For 1991 Ferrari's new car, the 643, wasn't ready until mid-season, and when it did arrive it was disappointing. Prost, fed up with the intrigue and in-fighting inside Ferrari, was outspoken in his criticism of the team, and of course the papers and magazines reported his every word. Ferrari took deep exception to his use of the media to fight his battles with them, and as a result he was fired before the final race. Disillusioned, he turned his back on Formula One for a season - and then came back, refreshed, for a final year with Williams. It was his most crushing yet: seven wins, 12 podiums, 13 pole positions, six fastest laps, and his fourth title. Then he quit while he was on top.

If Stirling Moss was the first professional, and Jackie Stewart the first modern Grand Prix driver, then Alain Prost was perhaps the first of the current generation of *complete* drivers, who understood that to be World Champion you have to be a winner not just in the cockpit, but in the motorhome too, and the press conference, the sponsors' dinner, and back at the factory. Having conquered as a driver, he set his sights on the even tougher task of running an F1 team, and in 1996 he took over struggling Ligier. In its five seasons so far, Prost Grand Prix has trodden a hard road, but Alain's perfectionist approach remains the same as it always was. No-one knows better than him that success in Formula One doesn't come easy, and no-one will try harder than him to get the results.

**Above:** Prost shone at Monaco, winning the street race three times on the trot, and four times in all, for McLaren. This is his victorious drive in the MP4/2C in 1986.

# Gerhard BERGER

When I'm walking around the F1 paddock, I'll bump into people I like, people I'm keen to talk to, people I admire, some people I'm a little in awe of, even one or two people that I may try tactfully to avoid. But one man I always greet as a true friend is Gerhard Berger - and I'm very far from being alone in that.

He's a warm, endearing individual, and he managed to remain so throughout an F1 career that lasted 14 seasons. He started in an astonishing 210 Grands Prix, which is more than any other driver except Riccardo Patrese (who started 256 in 17 years). While he wasn't a superstar in the Prost/Senna/Schumacher league, Gerhard would surely have won more than his creditable 10 Grand Prix victories if it hadn't been his lot to be team-mate to Mansell and, for three seasons, Senna.

Gerhard has always been a character, rather in the James Hunt mould. He is no respecter of persons: his practical jokes are notorious, and not always very funny, but the opposite sex have always seemed to find him irresistible. He is also one very shrewd operator. He made himself one of the richest men on the grid by managing himself and doing all his own deals, meanwhile managing to run a successful trucking business on the side. Now he's very much back in the swim as competitions boss of BMW, the engine partners of Williams. And still he's one of the nicest chaps in Formula One.

Gerhard's F1 career started bang in the middle of the turbo era, and his first two full seasons were spent with BMW power, in 1985 with Arrows with little result, and then in 1986

with Benetton. He earned his first podium at Imola, and then went on to score the team's maiden victory in Mexico City. Then came the call from Ferrari.

In all Gerhard drove for Maranello for six seasons, in two blocks of three. In his first year there he won the two final races of the season in Japan and Australia, both times from pole position. Then in 1988, just after Enzo Ferrari's death, he led an historic one-two at Monza, which gave him a place for ever in the hearts of the *tifosi*. He finished third in the World Championship, a position he was to equal twice more but never to better. There was another win in Portugal in 1989, but he had a huge fiery accident at Imola from which he was lucky to escape with only minor injuries.

For 1990 he left Ferrari and Mansell's shadow to sign a three-year contract with McLaren, but that paired him with Ayrton Senna. It took a man of Gerhard's character to cope with life alongside the fastest man in the world, but cope with it he did. Not only that: he apparently managed to teach the single-minded, straight-faced Senna how to relax and have some fun, and they became close friends as well as

team-mates. At McLaren Gerhard had a string of podiums - 18 of them - but it wasn't until Japan 1991, when Senna, having already clinched the 1991 title, moved aside on Ron Dennis' instruction that he scored a win. He also won the 1992 Canadian GP after Senna stopped with electrical trouble; and, helped by clever tyre tactics, the Australian round at the end of the year.

Gerhard probably got closer to Ayrton Senna than almost anyone, so he felt his tragic death in May 1994 very keenly, as well as that of his countryman and friend Roland Ratzenberger the same weekend. In fact, for a while he contemplated giving up racing altogether. He favoured me with the only definitive interview he ever gave on TV about his friendship and working relationship with Senna, "because, Murray," he said, "the BBC will treat it

responsibly and not try to make money out of it."

By that time Gerhard was back at Ferrari for his second three seasons, which brought a win at Hockenheim in 1994 and 12 more podiums, but the team was not at its strongest. Then, as Schumacher moved from Benetton to Ferrari for 1996, Gerhard returned to Benetton alongside his old Ferrari team-mate Jean Alesi. His last year as an F1 driver was 1997, and it was a hard one: he missed three races because of a sinus infection, and then his father was tragically killed in an air crash. Benetton boss Flavio Briatore made no secret of the fact that he wanted Berger to stand aside for a rising young hotshoe, so Gerhard angrily announced his retirement before the German Grand Prix - and then galvanised the team by earning pole position, winning the race and setting fastest lap. That weekend, Gerhard was certainly a hero.

**Above**: The last of Berger's five Grand Prix wins for Scuderia Ferrari came in the 1994 German Grand Prix at Hockenheim, when he led from pole position to chequered flag in the 412T1B.

**Far left**: After 14 seasons as a driver, the shrewd Gerhard Berger is still in F1, looking after BMW's interests.

# *Martin* BRUNDLE

## MURRAY'S NOTES

• *A very good driver who was never quite in the position to maximise his chances - either he was in the wrong car, or he had Schumacher as a team-mate. With the right seat, he would have certainly been a Grand Prix winner*

• *A highly intelligent, analytical driver, and a pragmatic realist: when his F1 career faltered, he went off and won the World Sports Car Championship*

• *Always a superlative communicator when he was a driver, and now putting those skills to excellent use in ITV commentary box*

## FACTS

**Born**: King's Lynn, England, 1 June 1959
**Grands Prix**: 158
**First Grand Prix**: Rio 1984, Tyrrell
**Last Grand Prix**: Suzuka 1996, Jordan
**Points**: 98
**Points per start**: 0.6

Martin Brundle is a very special bloke, as I have good reason to know. He may never have won a Grand Prix, but I regard that as being just as much an unjustified quirk of Formula One as the fact that Stirling Moss never won a World Championship. And he came near a few times. When Michael Schumacher retired from the 2000 Monaco Grand Prix, allowing his friend David Coulthard to score a magnificent win, Martin said with a rueful grin: "I wish Schuey's rear suspension had broken in 1994!" - because that was when Martin's McLaren finished second to Schumacher's Benetton around the punishing street circuit.

As I've already said, I've been lucky enough to have commentated for so long that men I knew, respected and liked as drivers have become my friends after they retired from racing. None more so than Martin, who never achieved the Formula One success that his talent deserved. It's probably fair to say that he only had one season when he was in the right team at the right time, which was Benetton in 1992. And that was when he had the misfortune to have Michael Schumacher as his team-mate.

I first got to know Martin in 1983, during one of the greatest seasons ever of the prestigious British Formula Three Championship, when he and Ayrton Senna battled for the title. In the early part of the season the Brazilian built up a big lead by sensationally winning the first nine rounds of the 20-race series, with Martin almost invariably second. But Martin never gave up believing he could beat Senna, and mid-season he started to do it. He scored six victories in the next nine

rounds. Twice they collided, on one occasion earning Senna a £200 fine and a licence endorsement, and once Senna went off on his own trying to pass Martin. It all came down to the final shoot-out at Thruxton: but that day Ayrton made no mistakes and Martin had to be content with second place.

Both drivers were obviously ripe for immediate promotion to Formula One. Senna was snapped up by Toleman and, in short order, went on to success with Lotus and glory with McLaren. But it was infinitely tougher for Martin. Nevertheless, he had a brilliant start in 1984 with the ever-underfunded Tyrrell team - fifth in his first race, in Brazil, and a magnificent second in his eighth outing in Detroit. He'd come through from 11th on the grid, and was beaten to the flag by World Champion Nelson Piquet by less than a second.

Then it all began to unravel. Two weeks after Detroit, his career suffered a major setback when he broke both ankles in a massive practice crash at the temporary Dallas track. And then all Tyrrell's results for the season were wiped away

**Right**: Eleven tough F1 seasons have turned Martin Brundle into the shrewdest of observers of the Grand Prix scene.

Below: Brundle's intelligent approach to all his racing made him a superb endurance driver. His sports car exploits were crowned by this Le Mans win for Jaguar in 1990.

by the FIA as punishment for technical infringements. Martin continued with Ken Tyrrell for two more seasons, stuck with the normally-

for Jaguar in the North American IMSA Series and winning the Daytona 24 Hours.

But there was still the lure of Formula One,

Far right: Of many fine drives, the British GP at Silverstone in 1992 was one of Martin's best. Team-mate to World-Champion-to-be Michael Schumacher, he not only soundly defeated the German to finish third but successfully resisted the non-stop efforts of the great Ayrton Senna, seen here vainly looking for a way past Martin's Benetton.

aspirated Cosworth V8 until Tyrrell got Renault turbo engines, and only picked up occasional points, like his fourth place in Adelaide in his final Tyrrell outing.

Joining the German Zakspeed team for 1987 was a hideous mistake, despite his brave fifth place at Imola, and so Martin, tired of tugging round at the back, made a virtue of a necessity by switching to Jaguar in sports car racing - with brilliant success. He won five championship rounds, from Japan to Jarama, and was crowned World Sports Car Champion, as well as driving

so he accepted a drive with the supposedly re-constituted Brabham team, now post-Ecclestone. The Judd-engined BT58 brought little joy, although on circuits where power was less at a premium Brundle's skill shone through, like qualifying fourth for Monaco behind the McLarens of Senna and Prost and ahead of Mansell's Ferrari. He scored a point there, and again at Monza and Suzuka (two points after Senna's disqualification), but for 1990 he resigned himself to returning to Jaguar for another triumphant sports car season, this time winning the Le Mans 24 Hours.

"MARTIN BRUNDLE IS A VERY SPECIAL BLOKE, AS I HAVE GOOD REASON TO KNOW."

A second year with Brabham, now with the Yamaha V12 engine, was no more fruitful, although there was a fifth place in Japan, but then came 1992, his one season in a top car. In the nimble Benetton-Ford he shone. At Montreal he should have won the Canadian Grand Prix, and would have done but for differential failure. In a really tenacious drive, he was third at Silverstone despite non-stop pressure from Ayrton Senna, and then second to Ayrton at Monza, ahead of team-mate Schumacher. In a year when Nigel Mansell was well-nigh unbeatable in the Williams-

seven finishes in the points for the French team, including a fine third at Imola. For 1994 he showed enormous determination, and a refusal to compromise, by hanging on for the second seat with McLaren when Senna went to Williams - only to join the team in its year of miserable failure with Peugeot power. Even so there was that magnificent second at Monaco, and third in Adelaide at the end of the year.

A second try with Ligier brought third at Spa but little else, and then for his final year in Formula One Martin went to Jordan - a nice

**Above:** Cruel luck lost Brundle almost certain victory in Canada in 1992 when his Benetton's differential failed.

Renault, Martin won 38 points from 11 top six finishes out of 16 starts, and was on the podium five times. It brought him sixth place in the World Championship.

In the end-of-season musical chairs, Martin found himself going to Ligier for 1993. He scored

move, because when Martin was battling with Senna in Formula Three 13 years before, it was in a car entered by Eddie Jordan's F3 team. But Peugeot-powered Jordan were struggling in 1996, a season in which Martin's fortunes weren't helped by one of the most spectacular crashes

ever in the first racing lap of
the year in Melbourne, when
he cartwheeled his car over
the barriers. Unhurt and
apparently unmoved, he ran
back to the pits and took the
restart in the spare car, only
to tangle with Diniz on the
first lap.

He qualified on the third
row in Brazil, and there was a
fourth place at Monza, but
when he came home fifth in Suzuka in the final
race of the season that was the end of 11 full
seasons of hard slog in F1. In 158 Grand Prix
starts he'd done good work for eight different
teams in all, including his single drive for Williams
in 1988 when, replacing a virus-stricken Nigel
Mansell at Spa, Martin was fastest of all in the
second qualifying session.

But, in a Book of Heroes, what's so special
about his achievements? Haven't others done as
well? Maybe they have, but many have also given
up when things were going badly for them; and
that certainly isn't the gritty Brundle's way. And
all the hard-won experience of 158 Grands Prix -
all the ducking and diving, all the strategic and
tactical thinking, all the hunting for the extra
fractions of a second - all that is now indelibly part
of Martin's make-up. It's why he has become such
a brilliant analyst of Formula One racing.

Admiration and respect, which heroes
command, are generated by a compound of
qualities: of which strength of character and
personality are crucial. Martin is streetwise ("I
have to be, Murray: I sell cars!" - in  different
Brundle-owned dealerships serving Toyota, VW,
Peugeot and Maserati). He's also direct, honest,

and cheerful. He has a great sense of humour, an
indomitable spirit and a very fertile brain, and
above all he's gigantically professional: he's very
much a team player.

I've always liked him, and
admired his gutsy
determination. When he
became my commentary box
partner in 1997 I rapidly
discovered that he is not only a
very engaging individual, but
also one of that very rare breed:
a top sportsman who can talk
about his sport - eloquently,
knowledgeably, authoritatively
and entertainingly. In fact,

he is the best co-commentator I've ever had, and
the easiest to work with.

When I reflect that he also, with his brother
Robin, runs that successful group of car
businesses, is a driving force on the British Racing
Drivers' Club, manages David Coulthard's
business affairs, has found time to try rallying at
the top level, and is a fine husband and a caring
father, I am left in no doubt that he is indeed a
very special bloke.

**Above:** Brundle spent 1993 with Ligier, finishing
in the points seven times and, with team-mate
Mark Blundell, giving the French team their best
season for seven years.

**Above:** Since 1997 Martin has worked with
me in ITV's commentary boxes around the
world and is the best broadcasting partner
I've ever had.

# *Ayrton* SENNA

## MURRAY'S NOTES

• *Awesome authority and near mystical stature allied to almost super-human speed and skill on the track. Took a record 65 pole positions - 40 per cent of the races he started*

• *Incredibly intense application and single-minded capacity for work, attention to every detail*

• *Ruthless self-belief and will to win led on occasion to torrid clashes on the track and off*

## FACTS

**Born**: Sao Paulo, Brazil, 21 March 1960
**Died**: Imola, Italy, 1 May 1994
**Grands Prix**: 161
**First Grand Prix**: Rio 1984, Toleman
**Last Grand Prix**: Imola 1994, Williams
**Wins**: 41
**Pole positions**: 65
**Points**: 614
**Points per start**: 3.8
**Percentage wins**: 25%
**World Champion**: 1988, McLaren; 1990, McLaren; 1991, McLaren

Capturing Ayrton Senna da Silva (his full family name) in words is not easy. He was one of the most complex, most unfathomable men I have ever met. Naturally serene and dignified, he radiated enormous authority and an almost mystical presence. And he combined one of the greatest driving talents the world has ever seen with utter ruthlessness both on and off the track.

Serious, broodingly thoughtful and deeply religious, Ayrton had a single-minded belief both in his own ability and in his god-given *right* to win. He displayed total commitment to every aspect of his chosen profession, and was capable of a phenomenal work rate. He devoted himself to doing whatever he did to the best of his ability, and his intensity set him apart from other men. In every way, he was a truly formidable opponent.

But he was also sincere, passionate, charming, awesomely eloquent in what, to him, was a foreign language, and devoted both to his family and to his native Brazil. This was a unique and immensely impressive man, and he has left his mark like few before him.

Like my all-time motorcycle hero Mike Hailwood, Senna led a privileged childhood as the son of a wealthy Sao Paulo businessman, Milton da Silva, who gave his son a kart when he was only four years old. In doing so he unwittingly set Ayrton on his path for life. Obsessed with becoming a racer, the boy ceaselessly applied himself to developing and perfecting his latent ability. He won his first kart race and then, with the dedication that was to become his trade mark, won championship after championship (but never the World Kart Championship to

which he aspired so fiercely). After eight years of success he was ready to move on: to Europe, and to car racing.

It wasn't easy. Ayrton loved his family and his country almost as much as his vocation, but he uprooted himself and, now 21, moved to alien England with his new wife Liliane. The marriage was to be rapidly destroyed by the pressures of their new life, but where Liliane wilted, Ayrton bloomed. In 1981, driving for Van Diemen, he swept all before him in Formula Ford, winning both the major championships. Moving up to FF2000, he was even more dominant in 1982, with 22 wins and the British and European titles. Emerson Fittipaldi and Nelson Piquet had shown that Brazil could produce the very best, but Senna seemed destined for even greater stardom. When he took pole position for his first Formula Three race, and won it, it was clear he was going to the very top.

So he did, in double-quick time. He had a fabulous season of Formula Three, fighting for the British Championship as we've seen against

**Right**: At work, Ayrton Senna rarely smiled. His whole demeanour was always one of unfathomably deep concentration on the job in hand.

"AYRTON'S OBSESSIVE
IMMERSION IN HIS
JOB WAS AWESOME.
NOTHING
ESCAPED HIM."

another of my heroes, Martin Brundle. He clinched the title in the very last race - and then went on to become what was, in effect, F3 World Champion at Macau. By then he'd had Formula One tests for Williams, Toleman and Brabham, and as soon as he'd crossed the line at Macau he was on the phone to Brabham boss Bernie Ecclestone. I know, because I was there!

But in 1984 it was with the also-ran Toleman team that Ayrton started in Formula One. It was a team with which he was never going to win - but, amazingly, he nearly did. At the Monaco Grand Prix, one of the wettest on record, Senna's control of the turbocharged Toleman was uncanny. The race was stopped early, but if it had lasted for just one more lap he would almost certainly have passed Alain Prost to win.

Ayrton had made his mark in his first F1 season, and now we saw his ruthless side. Without notifying Toleman team boss Alex Hawkridge, he signed for Lotus - and was mortified to be suspended from the Italian Grand Prix for doing so. But, from his point of view, it mattered little. He was taking a giant step forward.

Ayrton's obsessive immersion in his job was awesome. Nothing escaped him. Debriefs with his race engineers lasted literally for hours. (At Monaco once, I waited four and a half hours to interview him whilst he went over every detail of the car and its performance. But he'd said he

would talk to me and, typically, when he was ready he did.) He amazed his engineers with his total recall of what the car was doing, how it handled, the revs he was pulling, how his tyres were behaving and what his instruments were reading. His tactical ability was also immense, and at Lotus his towering talent came into its own. The switch to Lotus put him in a competitive car, and at once he showed he could beat the likes of Lauda, Prost, Mansell, Piquet, Alboreto and Berger. His first win was a dominant drive in appalling conditions in the 1985 Portuguese Grand Prix, and one of his career finest came against Nigel Mansell's Williams at Jerez in 1986, taking the flag just fourteen thousandths of a second in front.

Six wins in three years weren't enough for Ayrton, however, and opportunity knocked in the form of McLaren-Honda. At Monza it was announced that he was to join Alain Prost for 1988. McLaren was Prost's team, but for how much longer against the ambitious, grimly determined and politically astute Brazilian? Not very long, was the answer, as one of the fiercest rivalries in the history of motor racing began.

Things were all right at the beginning. McLaren were so dominant in 1988 that they only failed to win one race. Eight wins to Senna, seven to Prost, and Ayrton's first World Championship. But the rivalry erupted into bitter acrimony in 1989, with Prost taking the title after contentiously side-swiping his team-mate in Japan. It couldn't last, and the Frenchman went to Ferrari - only for the same thing to happen again in Japan. This time the collision was Senna's doing, in frighteningly dangerous circumstances, and for me he became a flawed hero when he stoutly lied that he was

innocent. It won him his second championship, though - and a year later he did admit that he'd lied.

Then came his third title in 1991. But nothing is for ever in Formula One, and by 1992 Williams-Renault were almost as strong as McLaren-Honda had been in 1988. Then Honda withdrew, and McLaren had to make do with customer Ford V8 engines. But, dramatically against the odds, Senna still took five brilliant wins: in Brazil, in unspeakable conditions at Donington, his record sixth at Monaco, in Japan, and at the season's end in Australia.

Tragically, that was the final victory. He made what seemed to be yet another career-enhancing move by joining Williams for 1994, but the new FW16 proved hard to get right. Senna took pole at the first round, his home race at Interlagos, but was outpaced in the race by new star Schumacher, and spun off trying to catch him. He took pole for round 2 in Aida, but was elbowed off on the first lap. Pole again for

**Above:** In 1988 Senna's McLaren won eight times and was second three times. This was one of the second places, at Paul Ricard behind team-mate Prost.

**Far left:** Ayrton's sensational first victory came in torrential rain in the 1985 Portuguese Grand Prix at Estoril, in only his second race for Lotus. He led all the way, and won by more than a minute.

round 3 at Imola, and he was holding the lead under pressure from Schumacher when he crashed fatally.

The reason for the accident was never established, despite a grisly enquiry that lasted several years and put cruel pressure on the Williams team. One theory was that the steering column had sheared. Another was that the car became unbalanced over the bumps going into Tamburello. A third was that the slow laps behind the safety car just before the accident had allowed

determined to stay in front. It may be that Senna saw in the German the first real threat to his superiority. But what actually killed him was a cruel chance: a detached piece of suspension penetrated his helmet. A couple of inches either way, and almost certainly he would have lived.

With his miraculous talent, Ayrton Senna's race achievements were almost as outstanding as his charismatic personality. From 161 Grands Prix he garnered 41 wins, including an unequalled six around the legendary streets of Monte Carlo, and

**Above:** British race fans will never forget the first lap of the 1993 European Grand Prix at Donington, when Senna went from fifth to first in a sensational opening lap. Here he disposes of Schumacher's Benetton.

tyre temperature, and thus tyre pressure, to drop, reducing ground clearance. There is no doubt that, with Schumacher on 20 points and Ayrton on zero, Senna was absolutely on the limit, totally

three World Championship titles. There were also a record 65 pole positions, 614 World Championship points - second only to his bitter rival Alain Prost - and podium finishes from very

**Left**: Qualifying the Williams at Imola for his last race. He took pole position for the 65th time in his career.

that, off-season, he would watch taped TV coverage of the past year's races: not, it turned out, in his native Portuguese, but "always with your voice, Murray". He obviously kept up with the coverage during the season, too. At the beginning of 1994 I decided to revert to the correct Brazilian pronunciation of his Christian name - Eye-eerton rather than, as the Anglicised version had it, Air-ton. But I don't know why I bothered. After my first commentary I received a torrent of abusive letters: why is Walker being so toffee-nosed all of a sudden, and that sort of thing. So for Round 2 in Japan I went back to Air-ton. Twelve days later on the Friday at Imola, two days before he died, I interviewed him for TV. He greeted me with: "What's happened to Eye-eerton?" I was dumbfounded. How could he possibly have known, I asked him, that in my BBC commentary from Brazil I'd called him that, and in my Aida commentary I hadn't? He grinned at my astonishment, and replied: "I keep in touch, you know."

It was the last interview I did with him. On that black Sunday afternoon at Imola, Formula One went into shock. The whole of Brazil was devastated. The man who for so many had been the greatest racing driver of all time was no more. His tragic death led to intensified efforts to improve Formula One safety, but for Senna it was too late. Now he rests in a simple grave at Morumbi in his home city of São Paulo, never to be forgotten.

nearly 50 per cent of his Grand Prix starts.

I have countless memories of this extraordinary man. Not only of his racing - although there are so many of those, like the first lap of the European Grand Prix at Donington in 1993. The conditions were atrocious, with a waterlogged track. Ayrton was fourth on the grid, and actually fifth into the first corner. Then, in barely a minute of driving like a disdainful god, he passed Schumacher, Wendlinger, Hill and Prost to lead before the end of the first lap. Later he came into the pits, saw his crew weren't ready for him, and kept going down the pit lane and out again. That was officially the fastest lap of the race: it was that sort of day.

Among my off-track memories are Ayrton showing me round the magnificent skyscraper in Sao Paulo from which his business empire was run - the merchandising, the Audi and Ford dealerships, and the Senninho cartoon character, profits from which were intended to provide welfare, education and opportunity for the young poor of Brazil.

So total was Senna's dedication to his work

"A DETACHED PIECE OF SUSPENSION PENETRATED HIS HELMET. A COUPLE OF INCHES EITHER WAY, AND ALMOST CERTAINLY HE WOULD HAVE LIVED."

# *Jean* ALESI

## MURRAY'S NOTES

• *A hard charger, volatile, vulnerable, explosive in and out of the car, but an honourable and friendly man*

• *Came into F1 as a talent with huge potential. Due more to ill luck than anything else, this has not been fully realised. Brave and determined, especially in the wet*

• *Drives his heart out whatever the circumstances, but does not always use his head*

## FACTS

**Born**: Avignon, France, 11 June 1964
**Grands Prix**: 194
**First Grand Prix**: Paul Ricard 1989, Tyrrell
**Wins**: 1
**Pole positions**: 2
**Points**: 239
**Points per start**: 1.23
**Percentage wins**: 0.005%
*(to French GP 2001)*

Jean Alesi, dark, brooding and handsome, looks like the matinée idol's interpretation of the Grand Prix driver. He often behaves like it, too, alternating dramatically between sunny good humour that lights up his face, tears of emotion, and a fiery temper. It has often been said of him that he drives with his heart rather than his head, and that may be why, as the most experienced man on today's starting grid with over 175 F1 starts, he has scored just a single Grand Prix victory.

So why does he merit a place among my heroes? Because he's an honest-to-god racer who always gives his all, even when common sense might tell him to ease up. He's an out-and-out racing enthusiast, and he's always been charmingly polite, friendly and helpful to me.

Alesi burst on the Formula One scene back in 1989, having been French F3 Champion and then driven in Formula 3000 for Eddie Jordan - and won the European Championship for him. That master talent-spotter Ken Tyrrell drafted him into his team mid-season, and his first outing, the French Grand Prix, went down in history as one of the great F1 debuts. He started 16th, and sensationally came through to second place before finishing a brilliant fourth behind Prost, Mansell and Patrese. He finished in the points twice more and, on the strength of only half a season, finished ninth overall.

He did a full season for Tyrrell in 1990, showing his skill on the streets by finishing second both in Phoenix and in his first Monaco Grand Prix, and by 1991 Frank Williams had decided he was just the man for his team. A contract was actually signed, and of course Williams were just about to start their most successful period ever, but Alesi was

not to know that. After protracted negotiations he let his heart overcome his head, backed out of the Williams deal, and signed for Ferrari instead.

Had he signed for Williams, his career might have turned out very differently. But, although he is a Frenchman, Jean Alesi is of Sicilian parentage, and the lure of the Prancing Horse was too strong. He stayed loyal to Ferrari for five seasons, but it brought him mainly disappointment. He was twice third at Monaco, the street circuit perfectly suiting his thrusting, attacking style, and in all he finished on the podium 16 times in those five seasons, with second places at Monza, Buenos Aires, Imola, Silverstone and the Nürburgring. But there was only one victory, in Canada in 1995. It was his 91st F1 start, and famously he had difficulty seeing where he was going on his final lap because he was so overcome with emotion.

He was overcome with rage when, at Monza in 1994, he seemed sure to win only for the gearbox to fail during a routine stop. Allegedly he got into his road Ferrari, drove out of the Monza gates and, still boiling with fury, drove it flat out until he got to the gates of his French home.

There were many flashes of brilliance, like his sensational wheel-to-wheel battle with Senna in Phoenix in 1990, and some inspired drives in the

wet, but there were wild spins and silly accidents, too. Nevertheless, when Alesi finally forsook Ferrari and signed for Benetton in 1996 along with his long-time Ferrari team-mate Gerhard Berger, great things were expected. Some great things did happen - eight podium finishes and fourth in the championship in 1996, five podiums, one pole position and third equal in the championship in 1997. But there were more crashes, collisions and mistakes - like the time in Australia when, with his radio not working, he forgot to look at the pit signals which were telling him to come in, and ran out of fuel. Benetton's policy for 1998 was to go for the younger generation, so Alesi (and Berger) were forced out to make room for Fisichella and Wurz. While Berger called it a day, Jean moved on, full of optimism, to the Sauber team with their Petronas-badged Ferrari V10 engines. But, while the relationship started well - he had a podium at Spa - it eventually disintegrated in acrimony. After two seasons he moved on to Prost, and once again

he looked forward to a new start with his former Ferrari team-mate. But he has rarely had the equipment to show what he can do - although at Monaco in 2000, where speed differentials can be minimised and differences in driving skill maximised, Jean qualified an impressive seventh, and ran strongly just outside the points until the transmission broke.

With more Grand Prix starts under his belt than anyone else on today's starting grids, Jean Alesi must now be coming to terms with the realisation that a Formula One career which started with such immense promise is now nearing its end. But I, for one, hope his ever-entertaining presence will be around Formula One for a while longer. He may be rather like a volcano always threatening to erupt, but if there were any justice he would have won more races than he has. I like him enormously for his honesty and style, and for his endearingly vulnerable character. If that weren't enough, he has a lovely wife, he grows good wine, and he loves his vintage Phantom II Rolls-Royce. All in all, a good egg!

**Above:** The 1994 Monaco Grand Prix was a typical Alesi day. Jean qualified his Ferrari 412T1 fifth, ran second in the race, collided with a back marker, stopped for a new nose cone, and finished fifth.

**Far left:** Jean Alesi's Gallic charm and Latin heart are a major asset in the cool world of today's Formula One.

# Damon
# HILL

**1992-1999** A PERSISTENT ENGLISHMAN

## FACTS

**Born**: London, England, 17 September 1960
**Grands Prix**: 116
**First Grand Prix**: Silverstone 1992, Brabham
**Last Grand Prix**: Suzuka 1999, Jordan
**Wins**: 22
**Pole positions**: 20
**Points**: 360
**Points per start**: 3.1
**Percentage wins**: 19%
**World Champion**: 1996, Williams

I've had some emotional moments in my years in Formula One, but none more so than the end of the 1996 Japanese Grand Prix at Suzuka. "I've got to stop now," I said, "because I've got a lump in my throat," as Damon Hill crossed the line to become World Champion. You see, I'd known and commentated on his illustrious twice-World Champion father Graham, I'd watched him from his debut as a promising motorcycle racer to his dramatic years in Formula One, and I'd come to regard him as a friend. So his success, at the end of what I knew had been a long and very hard road, was very special to me.

Being the son of a famous father can be a mixed blessing, and in Damon's case it was especially so as he struggled to progress, constantly being compared with his Dad. Graham was always seen not as a natural genius, like Jim Clark, but as someone with indomitable determination and a huge capacity for hard work. Damon was the same. At 14, emerging from childhood, his privileged life was shattered by Graham's tragic death in an air crash. Suddenly things were very hard for the Hill family. But where there's a will there's a way. Damon's passion was motorbikes (he's still a massive enthusiast) and in 1984, with hard-won experience from going it alone, he became 350cc Clubmans Champion at Brands Hatch.

Then, thanks to his mother Bette, he took a course at the Winfield Racing School in France, and did well. Being Graham's son was helpful now, as doors opened for him that might not have opened for others. Formula Ford led to Formula Three, and thence to Formula 3000.

There were wins, but no championships. "He's a grafter, just like his dad," people said, but he was a lot more than that, and he was to outshine Graham in Formula One.

Damon is an intense, industrious and awesomely determined chap. He is also a witty, modest Englishman and a fine and loving father, is sensitive, kind, decent, honest and courteous, and has a dry sense of humour. But he is no pushover. In an immensely competitive environment his F3000 achievements impressed Frank Williams enough to sign him as test driver for the Williams team in 1991. His skill, patient dedication and mechanical sympathy gained him respect, and in 1993 he got his reward. Mansell was out and Hill was in, as number two to Alain Prost.

In his very first year, against Prost, Senna, Schumacher and the rest, he took three superb victories in succession, but his second season was traumatic. Prost had retired, to be replaced by Ayrton Senna, but at Imola, in only the third race of the year, the great Brazilian crashed his Williams and died. Amidst the deepest gloom

**Right**: Damon Hill came late to Formula One, but dogged persistence made him the first World Champion son of a Champion father.

and despair it fell to the comparatively raw Hill to rally and lead the shattered team - which he did magnificently.

Four weeks after that dreadful day at Imola, he won in Spain. Then, in the most contentious and emotional season that I can recall, he went on

leading home Schumacher in torrential rain by 3.4 seconds.

So the Englishman arrived in Australia for the last race of the year just one point adrift of the German. But it all went pear-shaped when Schumacher made a mistake, went off the road,

**Above**: Going to the top. Damon swings the Williams-Renault FW18 through the Suzuka chicane on his way to his eighth Grand Prix win of the year, and the 1996 world title.

**Far right**: Hill's final victory was another for the history books. At Spa in 1998 he scored the first Jordan Grand Prix win, leading home team-mate Ralf Schumacher.

to do something his father never did: he won the British Grand Prix, to make himself the hero of Britain, which had fallen for his fighting spirit and tenacious personality. Then his rival Michael Schumacher was disqualified from his Spa win, and had to sit out a two-race ban, so Damon added three more wins. But he beat the Benetton driver fair and square in the penultimate round in Japan, scoring a simply magnificent victory and

came on again to clout the closely-following Hill, and put them both out. That notorious collision cost Hill the title.

So pick yourself up and dust yourself off, which is what Damon did. But 1995 wasn't good. Four wins, yes, but problems with the car, two more major collisions with Schumacher, and overwhelming pressure from the media and sponsors: second again in the championship.

Then came 1996, which was to be his best and, ironically, his worst season. It was his best because, by magnificently winning eight of the 16 races in the superb Williams-Renault FW18, he became Formula One's only World Champion son of a World Champion driver. But it was also his worst because, amazingly, Frank Williams had secretly decided to fire him at the end of the year and replace him with Heinz-Harald Frentzen (which turned out to be not a very good idea at all). Damon was left to read, incredulously, about his coming dismissal in Formula One's weekly bible, *Autosport*. And from then on, with one or two exceptions, his career went downhill.

For 1997 he signed to drive for Arrows, a team with absolutely no hope of victory - or so it seemed. But Damon's drive in Hungary was pure magic. Against all odds he was an astounding third on the grid, and when he swept past Michael Schumacher's Ferrari to take the lead on lap 11 I nearly went through the roof of the commentary box. But sadly the fairy story wasn't to come true. A wonky throttle demoted him to second on the very last lap.

Damon's last two years in Formula One, and his 22nd Grand Prix victory, were with Jordan. In 1998 the team was still struggling to succeed, and at Spa they did so at last. In a wet race which saw him at his very best, Damon took an emotional victory for a team that had never won before, silencing his critics who maintained that he had only won at Williams because he was in the best car.

But by 1999 the fire was almost out. After nearly 20 years of racing he was now a very rich man. With his charming wife Georgie, four children and other interests to draw his attention, Damon decided there was more to life than motor-racing. So, at the end of a lacklustre season laced with retirements, indecision and acrimony, he called it a day. It was a messy end to a great and glorious career.

No-one, but no-one, in Formula One has ever been liked and respected more than Damon Hill. His nation honoured him and his public adored him. He is one of the nicest blokes who ever drew breath, and he can be immensely proud of his motor-sporting achievements. He's left me with some nice memories, too, and not only on the track: that Pizza Hut commercial was great fun to do, and I was proud that he wanted to be my chauffeur to my *This is Your Life* programme.

We won't be seeing his famous blue helmet any more, with those knitted black brows and the intense brown eyes burning behind the visor. But I hope we haven't seen the last of him.

"WE WON'T BE SEEING HIS FAMOUS BLUE HELMET ANY MORE, WITH THOSE KNITTED BLACK BROWS AND THE INTENSE BROWN EYES BURNING BEHIND THE VISOR."

# Michael SCHUMACHER

**1991- TODAY'S TOP MAN**

Not altogether by chance, I was standing in the Jordan garage at the 1991 Belgian Grand Prix when Michael Schumacher got into his car to qualify. Just like everyone else, I wanted to see how this young German first-timer was going to get on. "Driving for Mercedes-Benz he's been a real flyer in the sports car series, and they've given Eddie Jordan a bung to see if he can cut the mustard in Formula One" was the story that took me there, and I was about to witness the start of one of the greatest careers in the history of the sport.

Slim and upright, obviously mega-fit, calm, very businesslike, confident, and having already achieved some remarkable testing times at Silverstone, he certainly looked the part. And by the end of the day he was the hottest property at Spa. He was to start his very first Grand Prix seventh on the grid, at one of the most demanding circuits of them all, beaten only by Senna, Prost, Mansell, Berger, Alesi and Piquet. Here was a man who was going places!

He was a former karting star who'd done Formula Ford and F3 in his home country and shown a lot of talent. In 1990, when he was 21, Mercedes-Benz signed up Schumacher and two other youngsters, Heinz-Harald Frentzen and Karl Wendlinger, to drive in their sports car team. Simultaneously Schumacher continued with F3 but went farther afield, winning in Japan and Macau. His fourth-row grid position for his first Grand Prix - on one of the most daunting circuits on the Grand Prix calendar - was a sensation, although his inexperience with an F1 clutch saw him retire virtually on the line.

Benetton bosses Flavio Briatore and Tom Walkinshaw were obviously anxious to benefit from this young man's urge to get to the top as quickly as possible, for at the Italian Grand Prix a fortnight later, Monza was in a ferment over the news that they had signed Schumacher - to the fury of an incandescent Eddie Jordan, who had failed to bind this glittering new prospect to his team. And Schumacher finished in the points in each of his first three races for Benetton. In his first full season he was on the podium five times in the first ten races: and then, 12 months after his first F1 drive at Spa, he was back there to beat Nigel Mansell's Williams by over half a minute and win the Belgian Grand Prix.

He hasn't looked back since. Double World Champion for Benetton in 1994 and 1995, he went on to lead Ferrari out of the wilderness to the promised land, and make himself one of the highest paid sportsmen in the world. There was no need for him to take on the daunting task of reviving Ferrari's fortunes in 1996, for he could undoubtedly have found a seat in just about any

**Right**: One of Michael Schumacher's most pleasing habits is his show of unrestrained delight when he climbs on to the top step of the podium.

team on the grid. But he rightly regarded it as a major leadership challenge, and he was the catalyst that took the proud Maranello team back to the top. For not only did he motivate Benetton's brilliant technical director and

**Above:** Schumacher's first World Championship came with Benetton in 1994. He won the first four rounds on the trot, and scored five more victories, only to lose his Spa win on a technicality.

strategist Ross Brawn to join him, but also that team's designer, Rory Byrne.

Together with team manager Jean Todt, Schumacher and his allies formed a quartet that slowly and methodically overcame Ferrari's shortcomings to be rewarded, in 1999, with the team's first Constructors' Championship since 1983. In 2000 he scored eight crushing wins and a total of 108 championship points, more than enough to taste his dearly-held ambition at last and give Ferrari their first World Drivers' Championship since Jody Scheckter's in 1979.

There aren't any bad drivers in Formula One, but there are precious few real superstars. The Fangios, Mosses, Sennas and Prosts of this world are very rare beings, but Schumacher is one of them, and he could well go on to become the greatest of all time. On the track he is not only blindingly fast but razor-sharp tactically, and so

fit that I've never seen him break sweat, even after the most arduous of races. In the dry he is superb, but his wet-weather skills are awesome, and his superiority in the appalling conditions of Barcelona in 1996 was one of the greatest demonstrations of sheer virtuosity I have ever seen.

He shares many of his characteristics with Ayrton Senna, the man regarded by many as the greatest of them all. Like Senna he is mighty in traffic, smoothly finding a way past slower men to lap them with the minimum loss of time where others get bottled up indefinitely. Like Senna he is totally on his pace the moment the race begins, and like Senna he is hard and ruthless on the track. Did he deliberately drive into Damon Hill in Adelaide in 1994 to win his first World Championship? I've never thought so, but people accuse me of being naïve. On his own admission he certainly took Villeneuve out at Jerez in 1997, when the championship was again at stake, and was severely penalised by the governing body for doing so.

Also like the great Brazilian, Schumacher works ceaselessly at every aspect of his craft. He is utterly dedicated to winning, and knows there is a lot more to succeeding in Formula One than just driving fast. So, fitness, strategy, tactics, every aspect of the car and his team, politics, mind games, personal relationships - he applies himself remorselessly to each and every one of them.

The results speak for themselves, and they are all the more impressive for the fact that, in F1, he has never been in the best car. Heaven help us if he is ever in a car which matches his talent, for it would make things very dull indeed. In his first full year for Benetton, as well as that Spa win, he notched up three seconds and four thirds and finished third in the championship. Year Two and there was a win at Estoril, five seconds and three thirds, although that only got him to fourth in the championship in Alain Prost's final year. Year Three, 1994, was the tragic season of Senna's death, after Schumacher had beaten him in a straight fight in the opening round in Brazil. But it was also a year of controversy and disqualifications.

Michael won six of the first seven races of the year and finished second in the other. Then he was disqualified from Silverstone for ignoring a black flag, won Hungary, and was disqualified again after winning at Spa because the under-car skid block was worn away. Then he had to serve a two-race ban, but he came back from that to be first at Jerez, second to Damon Hill in Japan, and so to the showdown final round in Australia with Hill and Schumacher starting the race a point apart. As is now notorious, Hill was chasing Schumacher when Michael slid off the track, and as he came back on again the two cars collided. Both were out of the race, and Schumacher was champion.

He took his second title the following year with an incredible nine victories - equalling Nigel Mansell's 1992 record of wins in one season - which were due far more to his driving brilliance and Benetton's superb team tactics than to his machinery. Speaking of which, amongst so many inspired performances, I shall never forget his incredible drive into second place in Spain in 1994, with his Benetton stuck in fifth gear for 41 laps; nor his magnificent Belgian Grand Prix win in 1995 from 16th on the grid.

From 1996 for four hard and long years Michael and Ferrari were playing catch-up, first with Williams and then with McLaren - and never quite getting there. But his first Ferrari win came in only his seventh race with the Scuderia, in Barcelona, followed by two more at Spa, where

he's always so good, and Monza, where the *tifosi* went wild, of course. In 1997, after five more wins, he was in a position to challenge Williams and Villeneuve for the championship, and arrived at the final round, the European Grand Prix at

"IN THE DRY SCHUMACHER IS SUPERB, BUT HIS WET-WEATHER SKILLS ARE AWESOME."

**Above**: Spa has always been special for Schumacher. He made his F1 debut there, scored his first win there a year later, and is seen here winning again in 1995.

Jerez, with a one-point lead. Controversy again, for as Villeneuve audaciously dived inside him Michael turned in on the Williams. They collided, and Schumacher was out, while Villeneuve came home third and took the title. The FIA held an enquiry, and decided to expunge all the championship points Schumacher had earned that year - though they left the race results in place.

Michael was second to Mika Hakkinen and McLaren in 1998, adding six more Ferrari wins to his total, and in 1999, after he'd won Imola and Monaco, it began to look as though he would take the championship to Ferrari at last. Then came the crash on the first lap of the British Grand Prix that broke his leg and kept him away from six races. But his recovery was rapid and in his comeback race in Malaysia he was instantly dominant, before waving Eddie Irvine past to help his championship chances.

Despite his immense achievements, Michael Schumacher is far from universally popular in Britain. His image is of a cold, arrogant, autocratic man. But, having interviewed him countless times, it is an image with which I could not disagree more. It is true that like Nigel Mansell, another of his few peers, he is seldom far from controversy, for he speaks his mind, and has also been associated with some contentious regulation-bending moves both at Benetton and Ferrari. I'd hardly call him charismatic, as Fangio and Senna were, but I've never found Michael to be anything other than courteous, cheerful, friendly, helpful, totally professional and, moreover, immensely authoritative and eloquent in what is to him a foreign language. What he says is going to happen usually does, and I find it refreshing that, when Michael talks in front of the camera, there's none of the bland and irritating corporate speak used by so many of his rivals. He tells it like it is (admittedly often with a psychological spin to suit his requirements!).

To me, Michael's sheer happiness and exuberance when he leaps on to the top step of the podium are immensely endearing. Watch him leap about and punch the air: it makes a sharp contrast to so many of his rivals, who sometimes look as though you've given them a fiver and taken back ten quid. We've all got faults, and so has he, but for my money he is without peer: the greatest racing driver of his era, and one of the very greatest of all time. Altogether a class act.

**Above**: Blasting out of the Imola pits in the 1999 San Marino GP on his way to his fifteenth win for Ferrari.

**Far left**: Schumacher leads the queue into Ste Devote in the 1999 Monaco Grand Prix. He won it for the fourth time.

"MICHAEL'S SHEER HAPPINESS AND EXUBERANCE WHEN HE LEAPS ON TO THE TOP STEP OF THE PODIUM ARE IMMENSELY ENDEARING."

# Enzo FERRARI

## THE LEGEND LIVES ON

If I had to name one individual as the greatest of all in the history of motor sport, I would without a moment's hesitation nominate Enzo Ferrari. No man, absolutely no man, has made such an impression, not only on motor racing but also on prestigious road cars over the last half-century. And certainly no man has founded a world-wide cult of such enormous magnitude. *Il Cavallino Rampante* - the Prancing Horse symbol - has a charisma that dwarfs every other car maker, especially when allied to that unmistakable shade of red, *Chiaro Rosso*. And it all springs from the personality of the man himself.

Ruthless, autocratic, a brilliant organiser and a manipulator of men, Enzo Ferrari was literally a legend in his lifetime. He never claimed to be a designer or an engineer. His genius was to bring together talented people and drive them hard, so that they built great cars, and raced them to the greater glory of the Ferrari name. The list of his F1 drivers reads like a motor racing Hall of Fame. Fangio, Ascari, Surtees, Hawthorn, Lauda, Mansell, Prost, Scheckter, Gilles Villeneuve and Michael Schumacher are among the cohorts who have raced, and won, for the Prancing Horse. And still any driver will regard it as the pinnacle of his career if he is chosen to drive for Scuderia Ferrari.

Born in 1898, Enzo Anselmo Ferrari had a moderately successful career as a racing driver, primarily with Alfa Romeo. Then, deciding his talent was greater out of the car than in it, he became manager of Alfa's competition department, before leaving to run their racing programme under his own Scuderia Ferrari banner from 1930. With the Scuderia, immortals like Tazio Nuvolari and Achille Varzi achieved some of their greatest victories.

Alfa Romeo and Ferrari parted company in 1938, and his severance deal stipulated that he could not reform the Scuderia for four years. But of course Enzo couldn't bring himself to stay out of racing, so he arranged to have his own cars built. In 1940 the first Ferrari, based mainly on Fiat parts, ran in a race - although in deference to his agreement with Alfa it wasn't called a Ferrari, but simply the Tipo 815 to denote its straight-eight 1500cc engine.

As soon as World War Two was over, Ferrari started building racing cars in earnest, and the first car that bore his name ran in 1946. Like so many great Ferraris to come, it had a V12 engine. So did the first Formula One car, the 1500cc supercharged 125. That made its debut on the Lake Garda circuit in 1948, and in the hands of future World Champion Giuseppe Farina it

"ENZO FERRARI'S GENIUS WAS TO BRING TOGETHER TALENTED PEOPLE AND DRIVE THEM HARD, SO THAT THEY BUILT GREAT CARS, AND RACED THEM TO THE GREATER GLORY OF THE FERRARI NAME."

**Right**: With few exceptions Enzo Ferrari treated his drivers as employees who were lucky and privileged to drive his beloved cars. He delighted in setting them against each other but with "Big John" Surtees, seen here with the great man at Monza, his manner was usually warm and avuncular. Rightly so, for he owed John a lot.

scored the first of so many great F1 victories. The first brick had been laid in what was to become an edifice of worldwide fame and glory.

In 1951, Ferrari broke Alfa Romeo's stranglehold on the World Championship when Gonzalez won the British Grand Prix. Remembering his break with Alfa in 1938, it was a victory that must have been particularly sweet for Ferrari himself. From then on, apart from the brief Mercedes period in 1954-55, the cars from Maranello more or less dominated Formula One until the arrival at the end of the decade of the British rear-engined cars. Since then there have been championships in the 1960s (Phil Hill, Surtees) and the 1970s (Lauda, Scheckter), and constructors' if not drivers' titles in the 1980s and 1990s. And now, of course, the Ferrari renaissance in Formula One has well and truly arrived.

Scuderia Ferrari is the only team that has taken part in the World Championship in every single season since it was initiated in 1950. It has won more victories and taken more pole positions than any other, and it commands worldwide affection, deep respect and fervent support in every country where F1 is run - or watched on TV, for that matter. Ferrari is still Formula One's yardstick for achievement. They have earned immense success in classic sports car events, too, from Le Mans to Daytona, from the Nürburgring to Monza. It is a truly astounding record, and it is due to the autocratic driving force of Enzo Ferrari himself. Meanwhile road-going Ferraris continue to be perhaps the most desirable sports cars on the planet - even though Enzo Ferrari himself always said that building and selling road cars was just a side show to help pay for the racing programme.

"I WAS UNASHAMEDLY AWESTRUCK AT BEING IN THE PRESENCE OF THE GREAT MAN."

Right: Ferrari in the Monza paddock with long-time acolyte and latterly press relations man Franco Gozzi.

There was tragedy in Enzo Ferrari's life, for his beloved son Alfredo, known as Dino, died of kidney failure at the age of 24. And many great drivers - Ascari, Bandini, Castellotti, Collins, De Portago, Musso, Pedro Rodriguez, Gilles Villeneuve, von Trips - died at the wheel of Ferraris. All this served to increase the enigma that surrounded the man. Even in the 1950s he rarely attended Grands Prix, preferring to direct operations from his office at the factory, and in his later years he was almost a recluse, although for many years he would make a brief public appearance on one of the practice days for the Italian Grand Prix.

He was always a man whom it was my ambition to meet, and interview. And in April 1987, when the Commendatore was in his 90th year and had little more than a year left to live, I did meet him at last. I was unashamedly awestruck at being in the presence of the great man in his famous study at Maranello, with the painting of the still missed Dino facing him on the wall, and a black glass Prancing Horse, a present from actor Paul Newman, on his desk. How on earth could I find something new to say to this great figure, who had been interviewed so many hundreds of times in his long career?

"Mr Ferrari," I said, "You don't know me, but you knew my father when you ran a motorcycle team in the 1930s. You used Rudge-Whitworth bikes, and my father organised their supply." I thought I saw a sparkle of interest behind the dark glasses he always wore. "Yes," he said. "I bought them from Signor Borrani, who was the Rudge

distributor in Milan." I'd got his attention! I have to admit it wasn't the greatest interview I've ever

**Above**: Monza 1965. Enzo Ferrari makes one of his racetrack visits to watch his star driver John Surtees at work. But despite the Commendatore's goodwill the relationship was not to last much longer. After winning the Belgian GP Surtees walked out following a season-long clash of personalities with Team Manager Dragoni.

done, because we conversed through an interpreter, but for me it was an experience that I'll never forget.

Enzo Ferrari died on 14 August 1988, aged 90. His name was, and is, one of the most famous in the world, synonymous with the car that just about everybody would like to own. By the time of his death the priceless business that he had built was controlled by Fiat; yet the old man's influence seemed to live on inextinguishably.

Less than four weeks after his death, the Italian Grand Prix was run as always at Monza. Ferrari hadn't won a Grand Prix all year, but that warm autumn afternoon Gerhard Berger and Michele Alboreto brought the Ferrari-mad *tifosi* to a pitch of hysteria as they scored a triumphant one-two. Just as he'd always done from his desk at Maranello, somehow you felt the Old Man was still pulling the strings.

# Colin
# CHAPMAN

"CHAPMAN WAS
POSSESSED OF AN
EXTRAORDINARILY
CLEAR, ANALYTICAL
MIND, A FEROCIOUSLY
IMPATIENT SPIRIT,
AND AN UNBELIEVABLY
GOOD MEMORY."

If love is blind, then hero-worship must be also, for there were aspects of the late, very great, Colin Chapman's personality and life that were considerably less than admirable. But the massive impact his tragically short career had on motor sport was such that it transcends his darker side. For a grey man he certainly was not. He was an intense, blinding light that shone bright to show the way to lesser men, and then simply burned itself out. He was a flawed hero, but a hero nonetheless.

Virile, intense, good-looking and charming, Chapman was not only a design genius but also an inspirational leader, a supreme motivator and an ingenious and gifted businessman who was always prepared to walk closer to the line of acceptable ethics than most of his peers. He was possessed of an extraordinarily clear, analytical mind, a ferociously impatient spirit, and an unbelievably good memory. Of his motivational skills, one of his ex-employees has said: "He could make you climb a mountain when you weren't sure you could climb a molehill." Perhaps he was too gifted for his own and others' good, but he will forever be remembered for an incredible array of achievements.

Anthony Colin Bruce Chapman was born in 1928, and as a teenager in North London he built his first car, a primitive trials special based on a cut-down Austin 7 saloon. For reasons that he would never divulge, he called it Lotus. More sophisticated specials followed, and when Chapman started to win club races - he was a highly talented and hugely determined racing driver - friends asked for replicas. On 1 January

1952 he formed Lotus Engineering.

The sports cars that came out of the lock-up in Muswell Hill were light, aerodynamic, and always bristling with clever thinking, and they became hugely successful in British racing. The first single-seater arrived in 1957, as did the first grown-up road car, the beautiful Elite, with its ingenious all-fibreglass monocoque. And by 1958 Chapman had put 2.2-litre engines in his F2 cars and become a Formula One entrant.

The first F1 victories came in 1960, from Stirling Moss in Rob Walker's private entry (Monaco) and Innes Ireland's works car (Watkins Glen). By 1962 Chapman's wonderful working relationship with Jim Clark was at its height, bringing World Championships in 1963 and 1965. Chapman never really recovered from the blow of Clark's tragic death in 1968, but the victories and World Championships continued: Graham Hill in 1968, Jochen Rindt in 1970, Emerson Fittipaldi in 1972, Mario Andretti in 1978.

And it was racing that Chapman loved. Despite the burgeoning growth of his other businesses - road cars, engines, boats, plastics,

Right: An extraordinary partnership between driver and designer. Colin Chapman in the pits with Jimmy Clark.

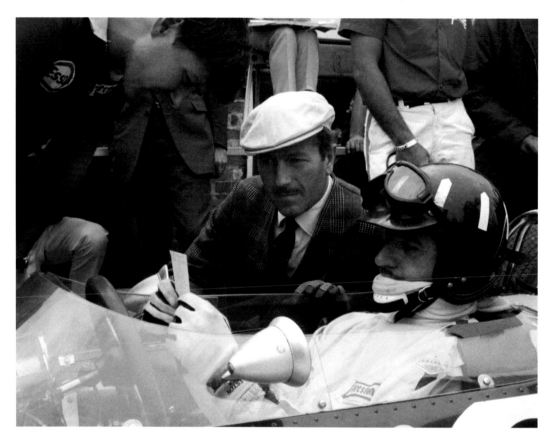

design. Over the next four seasons in the 25 and its successor, the 33, Jim Clark started 39 Grands Prix, 23 times from pole, led 30 of them and won 19. The 1967 Lotus 49 used its Cosworth DFV engine as a structural member, and that too was universally copied. The wedge-shaped Lotus 72 won Grands Prix over a five-year period from 1970 to 1974. In 1971 Chapman experimented with gas turbine power in Formula One with the

**Above:** After Clark's death, Chapman worked with Graham Hill to win another pair of Drivers' and Constructors' Championships.

engineering research - he would always be in the pits at every Grand Prix, running his team and controlling everything from race strategy to the design of the smallest modification. And it was his entrepreneurial acumen that brought Players into Formula One sponsorship in 1968, at a stroke consigning British Racing Green to the waste basket and opening the door to billions of pounds of tobacco money that would make Formula One rich beyond its wildest dreams over the next three decades.

But it is for his innovative thinking that Chapman will be remembered. His cars were always light, always elegant, often fragile. Time and again they broke new ground which would then be followed by other racing cars designers. The Lotus 25 first appeared in 1962 and, with its slender shape, monocoque construction and reclining cockpit, it revolutionised racing car

56B. The brilliant ground-effects concept of the Types 78 and 79, with their sliding side skirts, won the Drivers' and Constructors' titles in 1978. The Type 88 twin-chassis car exploited the aerodynamic regulations so ingeniously that it was banned.

Chapman's talents weren't just confined to Lotus. In the 1950s, his chassis skills helped put Vanwall and BRM back on track when their engines were good but their cars were not. And outside Formula One he conquered Indianapolis, revolutionising the thinking of the American speedway establishment just as he had in F1.

The row over the 88 was a huge blow to Chapman. He was convinced the car was legal, and perhaps for the first time his love of Formula One was shaken. While all this was happening, his other businesses were coming under more and more strain. At its peak, Lotus Cars had been producing 3000 vehicles a year, but in 1982 fewer than 500 were built. The road car business was now operating at a loss, and a major loan from American Express was due for repayment. The boat businesses had been wound up. Meanwhile, Lotus had been involved in development work for John De Lorean's ill-fated road car project, and Chapman had to answer probing questions from shareholders about why payment for this work had been routed through a Swiss-based company.

On 15 December 1982 Colin and his faithful finance director Fred Bushell flew to Paris for an FIA meeting, returning that evening. After a bumpy flight they landed at the Lotus factory at Hethel at almost midnight, and went their separate ways home. In the early hours of the morning Chapman suffered a massive heart attack, and was dead. He was 54 years old.

Tough and demanding, ruthless and impatient, and willing to cut corners to satisfy his enormous ambition, Colin Chapman had a greater influence on racing car design than anyone else in the history of Formula One. For my money, despite his shortcomings, he was a real hero.

**Below**: Another partnership that brought Drivers' and Constructors' titles was with Mario Andretti, who did four seasons with Chapman.

# Ken
# TYRRELL

## ONE OF THE OLD SCHOOL

Ken Tyrrell played an uninterrupted part in the motor-racing scene across five decades, and was a Formula One entrant for 31 years. He has always struck me as an archetypal Englishman: bluff, direct, cheerful, shrewd, honest, a man who has always spoken his mind, and a man whose enthusiasm for motor sport was at the heart of all he did in racing. In his early days as a Formula One entrant he achieved amazing success - three World Drivers' Championships in his first six seasons - but for its last 15 years in F1 the Tyrrell team failed to score a single victory. Yet Ken's status in the sport always rose far beyond mere results. It is because he, of all people, stood for the traditional sporting qualities of motor racing that he is unquestionably one of my heroes.

Ken was a Surrey timber merchant who raced in the 1950s for fun, both in Formula Three and Formula Two. Then he started to enter cars for others to drive, and discovered he had a remarkable talent for team management. When he was setting up the official Cooper Formula Three team for 1964, a friend advised him to test a young Scot called Jackie Stewart. Jackie had never driven a single-seater before, but he proved to be quicker in the F3 car than Cooper's works F1 driver of the day, Bruce McLaren. Ken hired him on the spot, and it was the start of one of the great motor-racing partnerships. It was to flourish and bring glory to them both over the ensuing ten years until Stewart hung up his helmet in 1973.

Ken ran Stewart in F3 and then, when Jackie moved into F1 with BRM, he ran him in F2, using a French Matra chassis. Matra were planning to move into Formula One, using their own V12

engine, but for 1968 Ken made his own move into the top formula, combining a Matra chassis and Ford's Cosworth DFV engine. By now he and Jackie were working incredibly well together, Jackie's driving talent and racecraft dovetailing perfectly with Ken's pragmatic organisation and strategic skills. That first season with the Matra they won three Grands Prix and finished second in the World Championship, and the following year Stewart dominated, winning six rounds and taking the title with ease. It was the first of three World Championships in five years. The mix of Tyrrell, Stewart and Ford was a magic recipe; but, when one ingredient was removed with Stewart's retirement at the end of 1973, Ken never again found the same success.

But he continued to be a major motivator in the politics and organisation of Formula One. His down-to-earth common sense helped resolve many a dispute between teams and circuit owners, and particularly in the pre-Ecclestone era he was a powerful force. His enthusiasms spread beyond motor sport, too. When we were at a race in foreign parts, knowing I spent my time on the

Right: Jackie Stewart won all three of his World Championships for Ken Tyrrell. They understood each other perfectly.

end of a piece of wire connected to a television sports programme back in London, he would pester me for the latest cricket and football scores, even though he knew that my knowledge of any other sport but the one I know and love was minimal.

As F1 budgets and costs soared, so the Tyrrells slipped further down the grid, but it was Ken's staying power and business acumen which allowed the team to remain part of Formula One for a further 25 years after Stewart's retirement. He was responsible for introducing several new sponsors into Formula One, who then moved on to become major spenders with other teams - not least Benetton, whose name first appeared in a Grand Prix painted on the side of a Tyrrell. There were brave technical innovations, too, like the P34 that his designer Derek Gardner introduced to an astonished world in 1976. Back then, nothing in the rules said an F1 car had to have four wheels, so the P34 had six, four tiny ones at the front and two normal ones at the back. It worked, too: it earned 14 podiums and even won a race - Jody Scheckter's 1976 victory in Sweden. And there was the angry dispute with the FIA over the use of ball bearings as ballast, which resulted in the

**Below**: As Ken Tyrrell's four decades as a team boss came to an end, Jackie's time as an F1 team owner was just beginning.

team's wholesale disqualification from the 1984 season.

Stewart was by no means the last young talent to be spotted and nurtured by Ken Tyrrell. It was his special skill, and he of all the F1 team bosses was always aware of what was going on in the lower formulae and who was looking quick. The man whom Ken was grooming as Jackie's successor, Frenchman François Cevert, was tragically killed just as Stewart was preparing to retire. Another youngster who Ken believed was destined for real greatness, the German Stefan Bellof, died in a sports car race in 1985 after less than two seasons with Tyrrell.

In fact, Ken was responsible for giving a first Formula One chance to an extraordinary list of drivers: Michele Alboreto, Patrick Depailler, Jean Alesi, Martin Brundle, Didier Pironi, Jean-Pierre Jabouille, Danny Sullivan, Ivan Capelli, Tora Takagi and Julian Bailey. Other drivers who benefitted from Ken's guidance and tough discipline early in their careers included Jody Scheckter, Ronnie Peterson, Derek Daley, Eddie Cheever, Brian Henton, Stefan Johansson, Geoff Lees, Jonathan Palmer, Mike Thackwell, Mark Blundell, Jos Verstappen, Mika Salo and Johnny Herbert.

After being an indelible part of the Formula One scene for more than 30 years, always ready with a starkly honest comment on the ways of the F1 world or a perceptive angle on the skills and potential of a young driver, Ken has now retired. He sold his team to British American Tobacco in 1998, and it metamorphosed into Craig Pollock's BAR outfit. His absence from the paddocks around the world seems very palpable, and I still expect his tall, hook-nosed figure to come striding towards me across the paddock and bellow: "Hey, Murray! What's the score?"

**Above**: The Tyrrell team brought many innovations to Formula One, not least the six-wheeled P34, which won the Swedish Grand Prix in 1976.

# Bernie
# ECCLESTONE

## THE BOSS

> "BERNIE INSPIRES LOYALTY AND RESPECT AND, LIKE HIM OR FEAR HIM, THERE ARE MANY IN FORMULA ONE WHO WOULDN'T BE WHERE THEY ARE TODAY WITHOUT HIM."

In its half-century Formula One has attracted some extraordinary characters. But none have been half as extraordinary, nor half as significant, as Bernie Ecclestone. It is literally true to say that the whole Grand Prix circus owes more to Bernie, as everyone knows him, than to everyone else put together. His drive, initiative, control and business genius have made what was a minority sport for enthusiasts into a global circus with television audiences measured in billions. There are few businesses in the world that are richer, or better run. And I'd venture to guess that there are *none* of the same size and wealth that have been built, and are still being run, essentially by one man.

Ex-racer, team-owner (of several teams over the years, if the truth be told), entrepreneur *par excellence* and enormously successful businessman, Bernie is tough and ruthless, with a razor-sharp brain - and a lightning-fast line in dry humour. He is, and always has been, the ultimate wheeler-dealer. "I don't make money," he says. "I make deals."

But he's certainly made a bob or two along the way - he's currently said to be worth two or three billion sterling - and you'd have to get up mighty early to be ahead of him. He inspires loyalty and respect and, like him or fear him, there are many in Formula One who wouldn't be where they are today without him - from team owners whom he has made millionaires to his past mechanics who fill major roles in the sport, like Race Director Charlie Whiting, the FIA's Herbie Blash, and digital TV mastermind Eddie Baker.

How has he done it? By having a brilliant brain. By being a natural-born businessman. By being a brilliant negotiator and a clever politician. By being ready and able to take on the world, whether it's dealing with the world's television companies, or with world leaders: he's made both the French and the Belgian governments back down over contentious issues. By being a gambler, who is prepared to lose as well as win (not that he loses very often!). But most of all - and I suppose this is a common denominator among all my heroes - by being, at heart, a Racer.

That's how he started, racing motorcycles as a teenager at Brands Hatch, and then graduating to a Formula Three Cooper. But soon his business interests left him no time for racing - motorcycle showrooms, car retailing, property dealing, almost anything that could be bought and sold at a useful profit. Still he remained close to motor sport. He was going to run his own F1 team in 1959 with his talented friend Stuart Lewis-Evans as driver, but Lewis-Evans' death in the 1958 Moroccan Grand Prix put a stop to that. He managed Jochen Rindt until the posthumous champion's

*Right:* Bernie Ecclestone as team boss, supervising the Brabham-Alfa effort in 1976. At the wheel is Brazilian Carlos Pace, later tragically killed in a light plane accident whilst designer Gordon Murray looks on into the cock-pit.

death at Monza in 1970, and at the end of 1971 he took over Brabham.

Like Enzo Ferrari, Ecclestone knew how to pick talent. With Gordon Murray's design genius and drivers of the calibre of Piquet, Lauda and Reutemann, Brabham won 22 Grands Prix during Bernie's reign, and two drivers' World Championships for Nelson Piquet. But even while he owned the team, Bernie was becoming an ever-more powerful influence in the organisation and running of Formula One itself. Eventually that became far more important - and far more time-

consuming - than a single team, and he began to concentrate exclusively on driving the whole of Formula One on to ever greater heights.

And he has done it, in effect, by himself. He has taken Grand Prix racing from a loose-knit and self-interestedly argumentative collection of racing car constructors to a closely integrated and formidably cohesive organisation which speaks with one powerful voice - his voice. He has his carefully chosen and loyal staff, but he takes all the decisions. At an age and with a fortune that might persuade a lesser man to slow down, he still works seven-day weeks and 20-hour days.

**Below**: Balance of power. FIA president Max Mosley listens, Ecclestone says how it's going to be.

Nothing happens anywhere in Formula One, large or small, without Bernie's knowledge and approval. It was Bernie who contemplated and fully understood the immense commercial possibilities of Formula One, and it was Bernie who manoeuvred Formula One into a position from where it could exploit and realise those possibilities. It was Bernie who saw that untold riches could be made if Formula One sold itself effectively to worldwide television audiences, and it was Bernie who realised those riches, for the teams and for himself.

Bernie's image is of a very hard man.

Certainly anyone who makes an agreement with him, and then fails to fulfil the deal to the very high standards he demands, will be neither forgiven nor forgotten. But I also know from several personal experiences that he is also a very human being. And then there's that caustic sense of humour.

When he decides to jack it in, who or what can ever replace him? He is an autocratic dictator who makes things work with unerring and immediate effectiveness. No board of directors, no committee could ever take his place. And that, from Formula One's point of view, is the only

**Above**: Ecclestone's is a slight figure physically, but even outside the world of Formula One he is acknowledged to be a very big operator. Here he is with portly German chancellor Helmut Kohl.

# *Gordon* MURRAY

## STILL WATERS

Great racing car designers don't bask in the superstar glamour enjoyed by great racing car drivers. They've always been happier to work in isolation away from the glare of the media, sheltering behind their drawing boards or, these days, their computer screens. But in Formula One you don't win anything without a good car. The man who can design a car that goes faster, handles better, is lighter and is more reliable can almost name his own salary - which is why top F1 designers like McLaren's Adrian Newey now earn as much or more than some F1 drivers. And it's also why they, too, are heroes.

It's a common complaint that F1 cars are too much the same. Everyone more or less agrees about what works best within the parameters of the formula, and the result is an almost standard design. It's a brave team that strikes out into the unknown and goes against accepted thought. When a courageous lateral thinker tries a tweak that proves unsuccessful, the others laugh complacently and say: What a dotty notion. I could have told him that would never work. But when he comes up with an original idea that does work, within a short space of time every other designer has copied it. Either that, or it's so effective that it turns the competitiveness of F1 on its head, and has to be banned.

In Formula One there have always been the true original thinkers: John Cooper and his rear engine, Colin Chapman and his ground effects. One of these uncompromising and ferociously clever individuals who is also a gentle, cultured and thoroughly approachable human being is Gordon Murray.

"PART OF GORDON'S SECRET AS A DESIGN FREE-THINKER IS THAT HE HAS NEVER THOUGHT THE WORLD BEGAN AND ENDED WITH FORMULA ONE."

Tall, thin, quiet, modest and calm, with a mane of dark hair and a fearsome moustache, Gordon was born in South Africa, son of a spare-time motorcycle racer. He built his first car, a Lotus 7-like club racer, as a teenage engineering student, and campaigned it successfully in local events. At 23 he came to England, found his way to the Brabham factory and got a job in the drawing office. He was still there two years later when Bernie Ecclestone bought the team, and instantly recognised the young man's talent. "I found him in a cupboard" was Bernie's reply when asked where Murray had come from. He gave him the task of coming up with Brabham's 1973 F1 car, and the result was the mould-breaking BT42. With its small overall dimensions and triangular-section monocoque, it was certainly different.

Then came the BT44 with its pull-rod suspension (later universally copied) which won three races in 1974, and the elegant Alfa Romeo-powered BT46, which used carbon brakes, on-board air jacks and, instead of conventional radiators, surface cooling panels - one of Gordon's

**Above:** Gordon Murray's razor-sharp brain assimilated his drivers' feedback (here Nelson Piquet) and responded with brilliant solutions that won races.

few clever ideas that didn't work in practice.

One idea that worked *too* well was the BT46B, the infamous fan car, which had a big rear

them in for a mid-race pitstop. This was during Gordon's zenith as an F1 designer. In 1981 Nelson Piquet became World Champion in the BT49C-

**Above:** Early Brabham days. Gordon in 1975 with the two drivers called Carlos, Reutemann (left) and Pace.

fan drawing air through a system of skirts under the car so that it literally sucked the car on to the road. The result was unprecedented levels of grip with very little penalty in drag. It won its first race, the 1978 Swedish Grand Prix, with contemptuous ease, and was promptly banned.

One Gordon Murray initiative which did totally change the face of Formula One came in 1982, when he had the idea of running his cars on softer rubber and half-full tanks, and bringing

Cosworth, and in 1983 he won the title again in the BMW turbo-powered BT52. Thereafter the Brabham-BMW star began to wane. Piquet's win in France in 1985 was the marque's final victory, and the revolutionary low-line BT55 of 1986, with its engine lying on its side, was not a success.

Part of Gordon's secret as a design freethinker is that he has never thought the world began and ended with Formula One. He has other passions: rock music, fine wines, fast motorcycles.

Having reigned as the most lively design mind in the pit lane, he eventually found that the constricted design parameters of Formula One had begun to pall. After 14 years with Brabham, he left at the end of 1986 to join McLaren as technical director, but he vowed he'd only spend three more years in F1.

This was a hugely successful period for McLaren, for the team won 29 Grands Prix between 1987 and 1989. The design of the all-conquering MP4/4 was primarily Steve Nichols' project, but among other roles Gordon acted as the team's race strategist, second- and third-guessing the race in the way that Ross Brawn was to do so effectively at Ferrari a decade later.

Gordon was now lusting after a completely new set of challenges to tackle. He found them in Ron Dennis' ambition to build a no-expense-spared, no-holds-barred road car, which famously grew out of a conversation between Ron, Gordon and two other McLaren directors when they were stuck at Milan airport after the 1988 Italian Grand Prix. Over the next six years, in a tremendous burst of brilliant design and

development creativity, Gordon became the father of the 230 mph three-seater McLaren F1, surely the most sensational road-legal vehicle that will ever be built.

Now he is focusing on other brilliant ideas - like a city car which will be virtually non-polluting. And you know that, whatever project Gordon Murray's incredibly fertile brain dreams up next, it will draw on the challenges and stimuli he got from his time as Formula One's design maverick.

**Below**: McLaren boss Ron Dennis, seen here with Gordon, recruited Murray from Brabham to mastermind one of his team's most successful periods. Gordon's design leadership, strategic acumen and calmness under fire are legendary but to many his finest achievement was the design and evolution of the superb McLaren F1 road car.

# Patrick
# HEAD
# *& Frank*
# WILLIAMS

### BETTER THAN ONE

"FRANK HAS NEVER
LOOKED BACK FOR AN
INSTANT: AS MENTALLY
TOUGH AS EVER, AS
COMPETITIVE AS EVER,
HE HAS CONTINUED
TO RUN HIS TEAM."

Down the years, successful Formula One teams have tended to be run by one powerful man: Enzo Ferrari and Ferrari, Colin Chapman and Lotus, Ken Tyrrell and Tyrrell, Ron Dennis and McLaren, Eddie Jordan and Jordan, Bernie Ecclestone and Brabham (or Bernie Ecclestone and F1 itself). The exception is Williams. Williams Grand Prix is jointly owned by Sir Frank Williams, who after a decade of ups and downs in F1 set the team up in 1977, and Patrick Head, who came in at the beginning as design chief.

Frank has always been a Racer. He drove in club saloon racing and then in F3 around Europe, building up a single-seater parts and sales business and then putting together a Formula Two programme in 1968 for his friend Piers Courage. By 1969 he was running Piers in F1 in a privately-owned Brabham, finishing second at Monaco and Watkins Glen, and in 1970 he operated the De Tomaso F1 project - only for Piers to be tragically killed at Zandvoort. Frank struggled on in F1, usually on the edge of bankruptcy, keeping one jump ahead of the bailiffs and running Marches, the Iso Marlboro and the first Williams before selling a majority share in his team to Canadian oil magnate Walter Wolf. But this relationship foundered, and for 1977 Frank decided to go it alone.

He took with him a young designer he'd hired at Wolf, Patrick Head, and a great partnership was on its way. Patrick came from motor-racing roots: his father, Colonel Michael Head, raced Jaguar and

Cooper-Jaguar sports cars with success in the 1950s, and Mike Hawthorn was a family friend. In 1978 the duo became a redoubtable trio when Aussie Alan Jones joined as the team's sole driver.

The places started to come, and for 1979 Williams became a two-car team with the addition of Clay Regazzoni. Patrick's elegant FW07 took five victories that year, and second place in the Constructors' Championship, and Williams was really on its way. In 1980 Jones was World Champion, and since then there have been six more Drivers' titles - Rosberg, Piquet, Mansell, Prost, Hill and Villeneuve - and eight Constructors' titles.

Right in the middle of all this successful activity, in March 1986, Frank was dreadfully injured when his hire car crashed in France returning from a test at Paul Ricard. This man who had always been dedicatedly fit, who was a bundle of non-stop nervous energy and ran marathons on a regular basis, will be confined to a wheel chair for the rest of his life. But Frank has never looked back for an instant: as mentally tough as ever, as competitive as ever, he has continued to run his team, and the victories and championships have gone on being won. Everyone except Frank himself realises this is human heroism of the highest order, and when he became Sir Frank

in the 1999 New Year's Honours, the whole of Formula One rejoiced.

All this time, Patrick has continued to be probably the most consistently successful design chief in Formula One. That neat, nimble FW07, which won the first Drivers' and Constructors' Championships for Williams, was followed by the Honda-powered FW11 and FW11B that during 1986 and 1987 brought 18 victories, a Drivers' title and two Constructors' titles. Patrick did much early work on active suspension in the 1980s - Piquet won at Monza in 1987 in an active Williams - and come the Renault-powered era of 1992/93 his fully-developed active suspension system, together with young Adrian Newey's aerodynamic thinking, produced a car that was virtually unbeatable. The 1994 rule changes did away with a lot of Patrick's developmental ideas, but Williams still won the Constructors' Championship that year and, but for the notorious Hill/Schumacher collision in the final round, could have taken the Drivers' title too. The team took both, crushingly, in 1996 and 1997.

After five Constructors' titles in seven years, the Williams team slipped in 1999 to fifth in the rankings, their lowest for many years. Now their new relationship with BMW and Michelin has heralded a Williams renaissance, starting with Ralf Schumacher's 2001 victory at Imola. Whether Williams is winning or losing, Patrick remains a plain speaker. In a world where it's often hard to get a straight answer to a straight question, you know that any question to the Williams technical chief will be answered with refreshing honesty.

As a pair, Frank and Patrick epitomise all that is best about motor sport at its highest level: focused professionalism and total dedication, allied with an enduring impression that they both still love what they do. Severally and together, they're heroes.

**Above:** Patrick Head and Frank Williams have worked together for 24 years to make Williams Grand Prix one of the most successful F1 teams of all time.

"WHETHER WILLIAMS IS WINNING OR LOSING, PATRICK REMAINS A PLAIN SPEAKER."

# Backroom boys & girls

THEY ALSO SERVE

"THE MECHANICS ARE A SPECIAL BREED. THEY WORK INCREDIBLE HOURS, NEVER SEEM TO GET DAYS OFF, AND CAN RARELY ENJOY ANY SOCIAL LIFE."

**Below**: Each F1 team, apart from at least two motorhomes, will have up to four transporters for its cars, engines and spares.

When the Formula One circus descends on a race circuit in Melbourne or Magny Cours, in Montreal or Monte Carlo, the population of the area is increased for the space of four days or so by probably more than a couple of thousand - and that's not counting the spectators. Running a Grand Prix is an immensely complex undertaking, and aside from the big star drivers, the team bosses and the wealthy sponsors, there is a large cadre of highly qualified, ultra-professional people who travel from race to race doing their own very specialised jobs. Without them, there wouldn't be any Grands Prix for us to watch and enjoy.

In my years of following and talking about racing - and in particular throughout my full-time F1 camp-following since the 1970s - I've been lucky enough to get to know, and call my friends, an innumerable number of these people who are

the very fabric of the sport that I love. Their names may not be household words, and many of them spend their entire working lives in motor sport without ever getting any public acknowledgement. But I don't think my book of Formula One Heroes would be complete if I didn't offer some of them a brief tribute.

Foremost among this group are the mechanics. In the early days of Formula One a car might be looked after by just a couple of lads, who would also drive the transporter to the race and back, and as likely as not work without sleep for three days at a time. The first time Team Lotus entered a car in the Monaco Grand Prix, Colin Chapman towed it down through France on a trailer behind his Ford Zephyr with two helpers in the back, while its driver, Graham Hill, followed in his Austin A35!

Nowadays each team may have 100 personnel or more at a race. The drivers fly in and out in their executive jets, and huge, high-tech transporters bring the cars, engines, tools, spares, computers and tons of associated equipment. While the team truckies drive the trucks, the mechanics fly home straight after the race, so that they can be at the factory next morning to start preparing for the next one. And, as a modern F1 car is so complex, the mechanics are themselves all specialists - engine men,

gearbox gurus, fabricators, electronics techies
and so on.

The mechanics are a special breed. They
work incredible hours, never seem to get days
off, and can rarely enjoy any social life. But it's a
labour of love: they do it because they too have
a passion for motor racing, and they taste their
own rewards when their car comes home in the
points. That's enough to make the long late hours
of work seem worthwhile - although, if their car
ends up in the barriers, it will mean even more
hours of work.

They're all heroes in their way. But there's
one I'd single out particularly, because his time in
Formula One began back in those days of trailers
and two mechanics per car and carried on into
the modern days of huge budgets and huge
transporters. Bob Dance joined Lotus in 1960
and, although he worked for other Formula One
teams at different times in his career, he will
always be remembered as a Lotus man. He was
still with Team Lotus when they ran their last
Grand Prix in 1994. To me he epitomised
everything a good F1 mechanic should be: not
only brilliantly good at the job, but calm,
unflappable, adaptable, good-humoured,
possessed of bottomless reserves of quiet energy,
and happy both to lead and to work alongside
younger men and allow them to learn from his
immense experience.

Mechanics get very close to the drivers in
their team - close to a part of each of them that
everyone else in the circus rarely sees. Bob knew
well, worked alongside and was trusted by a
string of greats, from Jim Clark via Graham Hill,
Jochen Rindt, Mario Andretti and Nigel Mansell
to Ayrton Senna. And, like all the best people in
Formula One - and this is a gigantic common

denominator for the half-dozen specialists I've
selected for mention in this chapter - his energy,
his dedication and his professionalism have
always welled up out of an immense enthusiasm
for motor sport in general and Formula One in
particular. Without that love of the sport, he
couldn't have done the job all those years -
couldn't have put in the hours, couldn't have
made all the sacrifices.

The love doesn't go away when finally you
decide it's time to stop. Bob is out of F1 now,
living in Norfolk not far from the Lotus factory.
For fun, he's restored an original Lotus Elite to a
better state than it probably was when it was first
built, and he's still working as hard as ever. He
played a major role in developing the superb

**Above**: Bob Dance has spent his working life as
mechanic and engineer to generations of racing
drivers from Jim Clark to Ayrton Senna. After
40 years in the sport, he now works on Audi's
Le Mans cars.

Audi R8 sports-racers that scored a clean sweep at Le Mans in 2000.

One member of the Formula One circus who really is a specialist, in every sense of the word, is Professor Sidney Watkins, the Formula One doctor. A high-ranking brain surgeon who happens to love motor racing, Prof spends every practice session and every race strapped into the fully-equipped medical car, in TV and radio contact with race control and with a competent ex-racer beside him as chauffeur, so he can be on the scene of any accident within seconds. His own life is at risk, as a potentially disastrous crash while being driven round Monte Carlo before the 2000 Monaco Grand Prix showed. In spite of broken ribs, Prof retained his good humour and worked on.

Several drivers owe their life to his rapid aid, and he gets to know them all on a more personal level than most. It helps that he's a fun-loving, cigar-smoking maverick with a wicked sense of humour. Ayrton Senna was a particularly close friend - they even found time to go fishing together in Scotland - and it must have been unimaginably hard for Prof that tragic day at Imola in 1994 when the call came to rush to Tamburello.

Formula One racing is, of course, potentially very dangerous, which is why the role of Prof Watkins, the other doctors that assist him and all the medical staff at each track is paramount. It also has billions of pounds of other peoples' commercial money riding on it - money belonging to sponsors, promoters, television companies. So, for every sort of reason, it has to be run efficiently. An accident may, first and foremost, result in somebody getting hurt. But it may also result in a delay that will wreak havoc on television

**Right:** No Formula One race or practice session can start until Prof Watkins is in his seat in the Formula One medical car.

schedules in most of the countries of the civilised, and not-so-civilised, world. And if there is an argument between teams about the legality of a car, which may impact on the result of the race and thus on the World Championship, the stakes are once again huge.

Much of the immediate responsibility for all of this falls on the broad shoulders of a cheerful, no-nonsense South Londoner called Charlie Whiting. Charlie came up through the ranks as a Brabham mechanic in the Ecclestone days, and Bernie with his unerring eye realised that Charlie was real talent. In 1988, in the ultimate poacher-turned-gamekeeper move, he became the FIA's Technical Director. As a street-wise chief mechanic, he knew all the dodges that might fox the scrutineers or get a light car through post-race weighing. Now he was in a perfect position to try to ensure that none of those things happened any more.

Nowadays his multitudinous responsibilities include FIA Race Director and Safety Delegate, Permanent Starter, and Head of the F1 Technical Department. As Race Director, he monitors every second of the action, and he must take the decision to deploy the safety car or red-flag the race. He also starts every race: the grid start is the most dangerous and most controversial moment of the entire event, and the starting lights procedure has to be carried through with total exactitude. And, as the FIA's top technical man, he must pronounce on

interpretations of the regulations, which means taking on the top technical brains in F1, and getting the likes of McLaren boss Ron Dennis and Ferrari team manager Jean Todt to accept his word.

All of which gargantuan responsibility he shoulders with extraordinary calm and good humour. He is immensely authoritative on his subject, prodigiously hard-working and a very astute politician, and he manages to command the respect of everyone who matters. Yet he somehow manages to be approachable and extremely

likeable. How, under all that pressure, can he possibly do it?

The media, of course, make up a sizeable chunk of the travelling Formula One circus. It seems there are newspapers, specialist magazines, radio stations and TV networks in just about every country in the world that are hungry to cover Formula One. They all want to come to the races,

"CHARLIE WHITING
IS IMMENSELY
AUTHORITATIVE ON
HIS SUBJECT,
PRODIGIOUSLY
HARD-WORKING
AND A VERY ASTUTE
POLITICIAN."

**Above:** Charlie Whiting's cheery smile belies his immense responsibilities for the safe and efficient running of every Grand Prix.

and they all want to talk to, photograph, interview and film everyone and everything to do with the sport. When the whole thing was lower-key, the drivers and the few journalists who went to every race were friends who travelled together and dined together. Now a driver who sets a better than expected qualifying time may find that a hundred media people suddenly all want to talk to him at once.

Solving this problem has created a new role for each team's PR representative, who acts as the link between a driver and the press. He or she will sift requests for interviews, make sure the driver

Right: Ann Bradshaw has been in and around Formula One for so long that she always knows exactly what's going on, in her own team and everyone else's.

turns up as agreed to speak to reporters and TV crews, and also pass information about the team's doings to the press corps. A good team PR is

usually multi-lingual, preferably both diplomatic and patient, and probably on friendly terms with just about everyone in the media centre. The best ones of all have usually been journalists or broadcasters themselves, so they understand the pressures of a deadline, and know how to solve the media's problems. If you're a working writer or broadcaster, the difference between a team with a good PR and a team with a bad one is immense.

Which is why it's always a pleasure to deal with Ann Bradshaw. Annie has worked both in motor race organisation - she was with the British Racing & Sports Car Club - and as a journalist, particularly on the rallying side: for a while she was Rallies Editor for *Autosport*. And of course, like everybody else who does a good job in this business, she loves Formula One. She was with the Williams team for many years, coping good-humouredly with relations between Nigel Mansell and the media, which more often than not were pretty strained. She looked after Ayrton Senna in his tragically brief time with the team, and of course Damon Hill. When Damon was dumped by Williams at the end of his World Championship year and found a berth at Arrows, she followed him there.

After a spell working in racing in the USA, she became head of PR for the TWR group. But the pull of the circus was too strong, and she returned to her spiritual home at Williams at the start of 2001, once again as press officer. With her sunny personality, her friendliness and good humour, and her masterly

knowledge of absolutely everything that's going on, both on and off the track, Ann Bradshaw is a huge asset to the Formula One paddock.

Among all those hordes of media who are helped by Annie and her ilk, there are journalists who come into the sport and cover it for a few seasons, and then abruptly disappear to write or talk about football, or current affairs, or the arts instead. But there are others who remain loyal to Formula One, and effectively spend their entire lives following it with devotion. Among the writing journalists, the doyen of this group must be Jabby Crombac.

Jabby is a Swiss by birth, but has lived in France for most of his life. As a lad he talked his way into being the European Correspondent for

the British magazine *Autosport*, and as a fluent English speaker he became in the 1950s the friend, helper and translator for just about any British driver who was racing on the continent. In the 1960s, when Jim Clark had to live out of the country for a spell for tax reasons, he shared a flat in Paris with Jabby. All this time he was covering Formula One. He started his own French monthly, *Sport Auto*, which became hugely successful, and after selling that to a large publishing house he continued to write about Grands Prix for magazines all over the world.

Jabby, an Anglophile all his life, dresses rather like a 1950s British motor-racing enthusiast, with horn-rimmed glasses, a flat cap and a pipe. He can swear pretty well in English, too. His memory is

**Above**: Jabby Crombac, with cap and pipe, has been a fixture in the press rooms of more than 500 Grands Prix.

prodigious, and he can summon up an anecdote, not always printable or broadcastable, about almost any Formula One driver, famous or

1960s also meant the arrival in the paddock of important guests from the sponsoring companies, and important guests of those important guests.

**Above**: Motorhomes go on getting bigger. Seen in the 2000 Silverstone paddock, double-decker edifices have become the norm: note the leaping cat on the Jaguar motorhome.

infamous, over the last 50 years. And even Bernie Ecclestone, usually no great lover of the press, has a good word to say for him. In 1986, at the French Grand Prix at Magny Cours, Jabby clocked up the incredible total of 500 Grands Prix, and Bernie presented him with a special award. He was, after all, present at Monaco in 1958, when Bernie, then still a racing driver, tried unsuccessfully to qualify an old Connaught. That's another of Jabby's good stories...

Finally, a word about that modern Formula One phenomenon, the motorhome. The arrival of sponsorship in Grand Prix racing in the late

Soon the switched-on teams who wanted to make their sponsors feel happy were laying on five-star lunches for them all. From there it was a short step to luxurious motorhomes, which initially gave the drivers somewhere to change, rest and talk to their team managers. But soon the guests were taking those over, too, and many of the drivers now prefer to debrief and change in the race transporters.

The motorhomes soon became an external symbol of big-budget success. If you wanted to show your team was doing well, you got a bigger motorhome. McLaren were the first with a double-decker; then Benetton followed with a double-width affair made out of two vehicles side by side with a central edifice joining them. BAR and then Jaguar joined the race to have the biggest, grandest corporate lodge in the paddock. All of these operations boast cuisine that would be the envy of most restaurants, cooked and served by staffs of extremely hard-working and invariably very pretty girls, all of whom make up a particularly charming and decorative group within the Formula One circus.

What all of this glitzy growth has done is hastened the loss of some of the smaller, friendlier sanctums which used to be good places for a hungry and thirsty commentator to take a quick break. Foremost among these, certainly as far as the British media were concerned, was always the Ford motorhome. While they were supplying F1 engines to several teams, Ford hospitably sent this vehicle to each European Grand Prix. Now they own the Jaguar team, the separate Ford vehicle is no more.

And that's a cause for great regret, because two of the nicest people in the paddock for many seasons have always been the husband-and-wife team who drove that Ford motorhome to each race, set it up in the paddock, and then cooked and served wonderful English breakfasts, as well as lunch, dinner and big no-nonsense mugs of tea at any hour. Stu and Di Spires are still running the same Ford vehicle, but they now follow Ford's international rallying programme instead. Formula One's loss is rallying's gain.

Di, the friendliest of souls, was always ready to listen to everyone's news and anyone's troubles. Not least because of those ever-available mugs of tea, she became a sort of unofficial Mum to the entire British F1 contingent - media, mechanics, even drivers. In fact, Johnny Herbert even called her "Mum." Stu and Di are just two more of the wonderful and delightful people I've been lucky enough to know through Formula One. If I ever find myself in the back of beyond on a rally stage, the first thing I'll do is go and look for Di and her ever-open tea-pot.

**Below**: Stu and Di Spires, custodians of the popular Ford motorhome for many F1 seasons, and still active on the international rallying scene.

# Heroic places

THREE GREAT CIRCUITS

In my years behind the microphone I've commentated on nearly 400 Formula One Grands Prix, at 41 different circuits in 21 different countries: from Anderstorp in Sweden to Melbourne in Australia, and from Long Beach in California to Aida in Japan. I've seen a lot of

different Silverstone from today's superb circuit, for the first Grand Prix in race-starved Britain after the war. With minimal safety provisions, the field raced round the perimeter roads and towards each other down the old runways at a cumulative speed of over 300 mph. The atmosphere was fantastic.

But the next year was when it all really began for me, with my first-ever broadcast for the BBC. The winner, Switzerland's Baron "Toulo" de Graffenried, took nearly four hours to do the hundred laps in his Maserati. Since then I've been to every British Grand Prix - including five at Aintree and 12 at Brands Hatch - and have watched Silverstone evolve almost beyond recognition. In 1950 it was a royal occasion, with King George VI and Queen Elizabeth in attendance, and the majestic Alfa Romeos sweeping all before them.

**Above**: Aerial view of Silverstone during the build-up to the 1997 British Grand Prix, with Copse Corner in the foreground.

great places and I've got a lot of wonderful memories. But, from so many locations, there are three in particular to which I'm always very pleased to return.

As an ex-World War Two bomber base, Silverstone may not be among the most historic or glamorous of circuits, but for me it is certainly the most evocative. I was there in 1948, at a very

But the following year those magical Alfettas were defeated for the first time when Froilan Gonzalez, the Pampas Bull from Argentina, blew them away in his Ferrari.

Silverstone has never been short of excitement as superstars like Fangio, Moss, Clark, Stewart, Hunt and Senna vied for victory. And, for me, there's no doubt about the most exciting of them all: Nigel Mansell. His sensational 1987 victory over team-mate Nelson Piquet, his stirring second place to Senna the following year, and the course invasion by his euphoric fans after his crushing fourth win in 1992 are some of my fondest Formula One memories. But for sheer drama, Michael Schumacher's 1998 victory while stationary in the pit lane will take a lot of beating.

After a period of uncertainty, Silverstone - owned by the British Racing Drivers' Club, of which I am a very proud member - is now certain to remain the home of the British Grand Prix for many years to come. But there's one event which

can't go anywhere else because the race and track are one and the same: Monaco.

If I could only go to one Grand Prix a year, this would be it. With its sun-soaked setting under blue Mediterranean skies, the royal palace overlooking the harbour with its glittering yachts, the expensive restaurants and luxurious hotels, and the must-be-seen celebrities, Monaco is unique. The dramatic street circuit twists and turns, rises and falls around the streets of the Principality, and nowhere else can you get so close to the masters of Formula One in action. Nowhere else can you practically touch their

**Below:** In 1957 the Monaco harbour was a lot less congested than it is today. The Ferraris of Hawthorn and Collins lie abandoned in the chicane barriers after that year's Lap 4 pile-up as team-mate Von Trips passes.

800 horsepower projectiles as they blast ear-splittingly by. The spectacle is breathtaking.

There have been changes over the years, but the essential character of the two-mile circuit, with its 180 mph tunnel, has remained the same since its first race in 1929. Imagine Caracciola in his mighty Mercedes-Benz, Nuvolari in his Alfa Romeo, Alberto Ascari, the immortal Fangio, Stirling Moss, five-times winner Graham Hill and Ayrton Senna, the greatest of them all with six Monaco victories, brushing the barriers as they rocket round the narrow streets. The teams hate the place with its congestion and cramped working conditions, but for the enthusiast there's nowhere like it for pure high-octane excitement.

But for sheer charisma, and an atmosphere that positively oozes history, tradition and memories of great men and great races, Monza beats them all. Specially built in 1922 in a royal park north of Milan, it is the stamping ground of the legendary Italian *tifosi*, those rabid enthusiasts whose passion for Ferrari knows no bounds. The grandstands, paddock garages and pits have changed over the years, but in character the place is much the same. Such is its ambience that the first time I went there, at that endlessly long right-hander called the Parabolica, I plucked a little flower growing out of a crack in the tarmac.

**Below**: The magic of Monza. The start of the 1988 Italian Grand Prix - and although the McLarens of Senna and Prost lead the field away, the race ended in an appropriate Ferrari one-two, weeks after Enzo Ferrari's death.

"Nuvolari was here," I thought, "and so were all the other legendary greats." I pressed the flower in a Monza Yearbook, and I have it still.

With its very Italian restaurant and its paddock shops selling motor racing books and models, there's an air of faded elegance and charm about Monza, especially the long-disused and crumbling banked circuit. But there's a huge energy too, for the whole place pulsates with enthusiasm and character. It is where in 1971 (before speed-sapping chicanes were introduced) Peter Gethin's V12 BRM won the fastest and closest Grand Prix of all time at an average speed of 150.755 mph, and just 18 hundredths of a second covered the first four home. It is where Germany's Count "Taffy" von Trips, on the verge of becoming Germany's first World Champion in 1961, lost his life, and where the great Austrian Jochen Rindt did the same in 1970 to become Formula One's only posthumous World Champion. It is where, in 1967, Jim Clark drove one of the greatest races of his brilliant career: after putting his Lotus 49 in the lead, he lost a complete lap with a puncture and then stormed back to the front, only to run out of fuel on the last lap. It is where Ferrari

scored their only win of 1988 by taking an emotional one-two just weeks after Enzo Ferrari's death. It was also the scene of Nigel Mansell's

dramatic 1992 announcement that he was turning his back on Formula One to race in America. It is a living shrine to a wonderful sport, and it reminds you constantly of its great times.

Silverstone. Monte Carlo. Monza. It would be hard to imagine three more different racing circuits, but all three of them are so much a part of the rich and colourful history and traditions of Grand Prix racing. When I walk around a lap of each of them, as I always like to do at every circuit on the Thursday before a Grand Prix, I can sense that history and those traditions rising up from the very tarmac under my feet. Long may they continue.

**Above**: The banked oval section of the Monza track was built in 1955 but was always dangerously bumpy, and hasn't been used for more than 30 years. It still stands, however, redolent with ghostly battles.

# Epilogue

Writing a book is hard work, but this one has been a very real pleasure for me. I have always led a full and busy life, first in my advertising career with broadcasting as my hobby and then, after I had given up the job, full-time as a commentator with all the other things that go with it. I've never been much of a chap for looking back and mulling over the past. So, in order to produce the book you're holding now, I've had to remind myself of all the people I've known in the world of motor sport, all the places I've been and all the things I've seen. It's made me realise how very lucky I've been.

Not just because of the races, the travel and the multitude of wonderful memories which I hope to write more about one day. Most of all because of the wonderful people that have made my entire life such a joy. Forty-eight years with the BBC is a very long time, but I enjoyed them

I felt immensely flattered, and the time I have spent with them has been no less enjoyable: particularly as I have been part of a team that I can say with complete conviction produces the best Grand Prix coverage in the world.

Thanks to the vision, leadership and commercial brilliance of Bernie Ecclestone, Formula One has developed in my time from a specialised sport in a few European countries with very little following among the general public to a mammoth enterprise which commands worldwide excitement and interest. It has been a quite incredible experience to have been associated with it all, and I certainly hope to continue as long as people want to hear what I have got to say, and I am physically and mentally able to say it.

The friends I have made and worked with are too numerous to detail, but there is one that I want to single out: Simon Taylor. The Heroes in this book and the memories of them are mine, and so are a lot of the words, but the rest are a joint effort, and I couldn't have hoped to work with a

**Right:** Authors at work on location. Murray Walker and Simon Taylor compare notes in the pits.

immensely, and always felt proud and privileged to work with what I firmly believe to be the world's greatest broadcasting organisation. When ITV invited me to join their Formula One team

more cheerful, helpful, knowledgeable and enthusiastic colleague. We both hope you've enjoyed reading it as much as we've enjoyed putting it together!

**pp. 4/5** Grand Prix gladiators listen with varying expressions of impatience and cynicism to the drivers' briefing on the grid before the 1962 Italian Grand Prix at Monza. From left, Roy Salvadori, John Surtees, Count Carel Godin de Beaufort, Tony Maggs, Innes Ireland (with inevitable cigarette), Graham Hill and Jimmy Clark, wearing protection from flying stones.

**pp. 6/7** The Reims straight stretches ahead as the 1958 French Grand Prix is about to start. Mike Hawthorn's Ferrari won from Stirling Moss' Vanwall, but down at the back is Cliff Allison's Lotus 12, which lasted six laps. Graham Hill's Lotus 16 is on his left and American visitor Troy Ruttman, whose Scuderia Centro-Sud Maserati 250F finished 10th, on his right.

**pp. 8/9** Today's master on his way to his first World Championship title. Michael Schumacher hustles the Benetton-Ford B194 towards his eighth victory of the season in the 1994 European Grand Prix at Jerez. Three weeks later Damon Hill beat him in the rain in Japan, but in the final round in Australia the rivals collided into retirement, and Schumacher was Champion by one point.

**pp. 14/15** Tazio Nuvolari wipes his goggles as he storms through the village of Gueux in his 2.6 Alfa Romeo P3 during the 1932 French Grand Prix at Reims. Under a blazing sun, Nuvolari averaged 92.2 mph for the entire five-hour race, with a fastest lap at 99.5 mph, leading home his Scuderia Ferrari team-mates Borzacchini and Caracciola in an Alfa 1-2-3.

**pp. 22/23** Ferrari team-mates: Juan Manuel Fangio leads Eugenio Castellotti and eventual winner Peter Collins out of the Thillois Hairpin at Reims during the 1956 French Grand Prix. The cars are Ferrari-Lancias, modified versions of the D50s taken over from the defunct Lancia team and with their pannier fuel tanks now faired into the main bodywork.

**pp. 30/31** At Monaco in 1956, Fangio prepares for some practice laps in a Lancia-Ferrari D50 V8. During the race he stopped with clutch problems, took over team-mate Peter Collins' car and fought back to second place, finishing 6 secs behind Stirling Moss' Maserati. Two of the five D50s Ferrari took to Monaco still carried their pannier tanks separately mounted: the others were now faired in.

**pp. 42/43** Stirling Moss always preferred to drive British cars, and had one of his finest F1 seasons in 1958 for Vanwall. He won three of the nine Grands Prix he started in the distinctive high-tailed cars, and was leading three more when the car let him down. He missed being World Champion by one point to Hawthorn, who only won one race in the more reliable Ferrari. But Vanwall were Constructors' Champions in this, the first year of that contest.

**pp. 56/57** The monocoque Lotus 25, with its reclining driving position and slender cockpit giving minimal frontal area, was a classic Chapman design, and Jim Clark exploited it to the full. Here Jimmy swings through Thillois Hairpin at Reims during the 1963 French Grand Prix on his way to scoring a copybook Clark victory: he qualified on pole, led from start to finish, set fastest lap, and was more than a minute ahead of the pursuit at the chequered flag.

**pp. 66/67** Airborne at Ballaugh Bridge. In the 1959 Isle of Man Senior TT John Surtees had a legendary ride on the glorious MV four. From a standing start he broke the great Bob McIntyre's Gilera lap record and then, in appalling weather, went on to win by an incredible 4m 23s. When I interviewed him, wet and chilled to the bone, he could hardly speak.

**pp. 94/95** James Hunt lucked into the McLaren team in 1976 when Fittipaldi left, and crashed in his first race. But from then on he drove the season of his life. He scored seven victories (including the disallowed British GP win), and his last-gasp third place in the rain in Japan was enough to beat Lauda to the title by a single point.

**pp. 110/111** Nigel Mansell spent two years at Ferrari, happily leading the team in 1989 and then less happily feeling under Prost's shadow in 1990. However in his last race for the Scuderia, the Australian Grand Prix, he had a tremendous battle for the lead with Senna's McLaren before sliding down an escape road. Senna later hit the barriers, while Mansell recovered to finish second to Piquet's Benetton.

**pp. 124/125** Martin Brundle's final Formula One year was with Jordan in 1996, when Eddie's team was using the V10 Peugeot engine. It was a tough year for Martin, and he retired in half the season's rounds. But when he finished he was usually in the points: at Monza he was fourth, and at Suzuda, his 158th and final Grand Prix, he was fifth.

**pp. 132/133** When conditions were difficult, Ayrton Senna's racing genius always came to the fore. In the 1993 European Grand Prix at Donington, track conditions were constantly changing, from damp and slippery to torrentially wet. It was one of those races where one man stood out head and shoulders above everybody else. On the opening lap he went from fifth place to first, and stayed there.

**pp. 146/147** Michael Schumacher is without dispute today's top Formula One driver. Here he rides a Monte Carlo kerb in the 2000 Monaco Grand Prix. Comfortably in the lead, he was robbed of a fifth win around the Principality by an unusual Ferrari failure: a broken exhaust roasted a rear suspension arm until it broke.

**pp. 148/149** Pitstops are an integral part of modern Formula One racing, and the pit crew carry a huge responsibility for their drivers' race positions. With three men per wheel, two on the jacks, the refuelling crew, the visor cleaner and the lollipop man, up to 20 people are involved in six frenetic seconds of activity. This Ferrari stop is in the 1999 San Marino Grand Prix, which Michael Schumacher won.

Far left: **pp. 172/173** Logistically Formula One today is an operation of immense proportions, involving each team taking tons of equipment to 17 races in 15 countries across five continents in 33 weeks. For the European races most of the kit travels by road in fleets of giant transporters which are then lined up in the paddock with geometrical precision, exactly as prescribed by Bernie Ecclestone.
This is the Imola paddock before the 2000 San Marino Grand Prix.

Left: **pp. 182/183** Monaco, 1999. Eddie Irvine hustles his Ferrari 399 up the hill from St Devote to Casino Square on his way to an inspired 2nd place behind his team-mate Michael Schumacher.